16

GO BIG
OR GO HOME

Center Point
Large Print

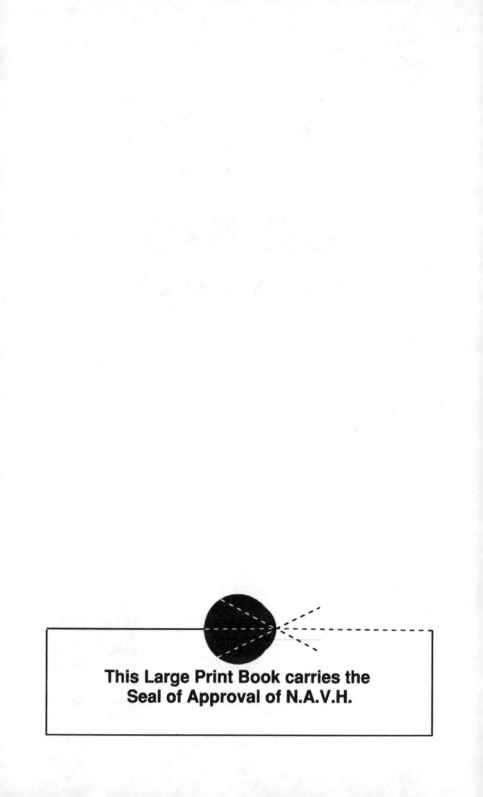

**This Large Print Book carries the
Seal of Approval of N.A.V.H.**

GO BIG
OR GO HOME

The Journey toward the Dream

SCOTTY McCREERY
with
TRAVIS THRASHER

CENTER POINT LARGE PRINT
THORNDIKE, MAINE

The text of this Large Print edition is unabridged.
In other aspects, this book may vary from the original edition.
Printed in the United States of America on permanent paper.
Set in 16-point Times New Roman type.

ISBN: 978-1-62899-994-5

Library of Congress Cataloging-in-Publication Data

Names: McCreery, Scotty, 1993 author. | Thrasher, Travis, 1971– author.
Title: Go big or go home : the journey toward the dream / Scotty McCreery with Travis Thrasher.
Description: Center Point large print edition. | Thorndike, Maine : Center Point Large Print, 2016.
Identifiers: LCCN 2016009439 | ISBN 9781628999945 (hardcover : alk. paper)
Subjects: LCSH: McCreery, Scotty, 1993– | Singers—United States—Biography. | Country musicians—United States—Biography. | Large type books.
Classification: LCC ML420.M341236 A3 2016b | DDC 782.421642092—dc23
LC record available at http://lccn.loc.gov/2016009439

To all those who dare to dream

I never expected to be anybody important.
ELVIS PRESLEY

True country music is honesty,
sincerity, and real life to the hilt.
GARTH BROOKS

I don't feel like God called me
to be a gospel singer.
He didn't call me to be a Christian singer;
he called me to be a country singer,
and I just happen to be a Christian.
JOSH TURNER

Prologue 9

PART 1: *AMERICAN IDOL*:
The Journey Begins

Chapter 1: Just a Normal Kid 17
Chapter 2: A Little Field Trip 39
Chapter 3: The Man I Want to Be 64
Chapter 4: America's Storyteller 89
Chapter 5: Prayers, Plans, and Promises . . . 116
Chapter 6: Hollywood and Homework 144

PART 2: LIFE AFTER *AMERICAN IDOL*:
The Journey Continues

Chapter 7: My Motley Crew 201
Chapter 8: Girls, Goals, Garner . . . and
            Brad 218
Chapter 9: The Greatest Gift 240
Chapter 10: The Thrill and the Joy
            (of Sports) 254

Chapter 11: ASAP—Always Say a Prayer . . 270

Chapter 12: On the Road 284

Chapter 13: Blessed to Be a Blessing 300

Chapter 14: Special Places and
                          Lots of Faces 313

Chapter 15: Business, Balance, and
                          Blessings 327

Chapter 16: Remembering the Moments . . . 343

Epilogue 349

Acknowledgments 353

Scotty McCreery: Quick Facts 357

Prologue

Everything changed when I first heard that voice.

I was in preschool when I discovered Elvis Presley in the pages of a book. It was a present from my grandmother on my fourth birthday. She was still teaching school and saw *Best of Elvis* at a book fair. She'd been a big fan since the 1950s, so she thought it'd be a perfect gift.

She had *no* idea.

There were six photos of Elvis on the cover. Most were shots of him early in his career, being mobbed by fans and performing, and one was from a movie clip, and there was even one behind a microphone in a recording studio. I was fascinated.

Two months later, my mother bought me an Elvis CD for Christmas. I finally got to listen to his music. My fascination suddenly turned into a bit of an obsession. I can't tell you the exact song I first heard, but there's not just *one* Elvis song you fall in love with.

There's just one Elvis.

It was 1997, but for me it was 1957, and I was a transfixed kid listening to this cool, exciting singer belting away about a county jail. I couldn't help moving my body and bobbing my head. Elvis was inviting me to dance along to "Jailhouse Rock."

It was an invitation I took. One I've never looked back on.

Five years later, when I was nine, my interest in Elvis had only grown. It showed up in everything, including a paper I wrote in third grade:

> When I went to sleep I was Elvis. When I woke up I was a human again. When I was Elvis I was dreaming about being Elvis in a concert. I looked just like Elvis. The songs I sang were Hound Dog, Blue ~~sued~~ suede shoes, Trouble, Heart Break ~~Houtal~~ Hotel, Teddy Bear, Don't be Cruel, Big Boss Man. I had to go all the way to Graceland. I do not know how I got there but I did. The way I changed is I drank something Elvis drank. I had a great time in Graceland. I had 5 concerts in Graceland. Then I woke up and I found out that it was a dream. ☺

The teacher wrote, "You really do love Elvis!" and "Great story!" on the side of the paper.

I had to go all the way to a land of grace and wonder, and I didn't even know how I got there. But I had a great time, even if it was just a dream.

But what if . . . what if it turned out not to be a dream after all?

• • •

A guy my age shouldn't be writing an auto-biography. This isn't one, really. It's more of a travelogue of all the cool experiences I've had and the awesome places I've visited in just twenty-two short years.

When I was sixteen years old, I was a normal teenager living in Garner, North Carolina. I loved to sing and play baseball. There weren't a lot of extraordinary stories that could fill the pages of a book like this.

But as so many people know, that all changed.

Since my incredible *American Idol* experience, I feel like I've aged ten years. Maybe more. In these past five years, however, I've hardly had a chance to stop and blink and realize all of the amazing things that have happened around me. All of the people I've met, all of the places I've been, all of the things I've learned. I love how the nation got a chance to get to know not only me but also my family, my friends, and my hometown of Garner, North Carolina. So many unbelievable surprises and blessings have occurred.

This is my chance to share them with you, and it's an opportunity to pause for a moment and celebrate this gift I've been given. It's not just the gift of being in the limelight; it's the gift of being able to do something I was born to do. The gift of singing for others. The gift of encouraging and lifting up spirits of anyone and everyone who dares to dream.

I also want to celebrate country music—from the classics of years gone by to the current talents out there.

Consider this book to be a party of sorts, honoring those who helped pave the way for me and those who have come alongside me during this journey.

It's been quite a trip. And God willing, it's the starting point for all the places I'm hoping to go.

Where did you get that voice?

I get that question a lot. I just tell them I was born with it.

Did you know you'd win American Idol*?*

That question comes often too. The answer is no. I didn't think I had a chance.

I did have a dream, however. Songs didn't just fill my mind; they filled my soul. I had to let them out somehow, some way.

Oh, this mystery train was comin' 'round the bend. But it wasn't long and black; it was short, bright, and beautiful. It scooped me up and told me to hold on for the ride. So I've been trying to hold on.

Maybe Elvis was right—maybe only fools rush in.

But as a preschooler, I couldn't help falling in love with that sound. That rush. That world.

I had a strange ambition in life during my grade school years: I wanted to be like Elvis.

And while I know there will never be another Elvis, just like there'll never be another Johnny Cash, George Jones, or Garth Brooks, I also know something else: God gave me a voice, and America gave me a chance.

This book is about those two things and about the amazing journey that began the moment I decided to say two words about this show I knew and loved.

Why not?

PART 1

AMERICAN IDOL

The Journey Begins

Chapter 1

Just a Normal Kid

"Contestant number ten is Scotty McCreery."

The applause is anything but deafening. I can count on one hand all the people who are cheering for me in the auditorium.

"I understand he has a nickname: 'Scotty Mac.' And he's always loved music. At his first-year checkup, he hummed a few bars of 'Bye, Baby Bunting' to his amazed doctor. Later, when he was three, his mother feared arrest by the Mexican police when she looked and saw him walking beside her, strumming a tiny blue ukulele he'd walked out of the store with."

The laughter makes me feel a little better. As Keith Branch, the talent show emcee, continues to share my brief bio, I think through the lyrics of the song I'm about to sing. As Mr. Branch continues, the audience learns about my love for Elvis Presley CDs and how I wanted to take guitar lessons instead of piano lessons. The emcee finishes my introduction by rambling off a list of accomplishments I'd have felt embarrassed to publicly share myself.

"Ladies and gentlemen, a warm welcome for contestant number ten—Scotty McCreery."

A few more cheers greet me as I emerge from backstage and step into the light. I'm carrying a barstool in one hand and my guitar in the other. I adjust the microphone and then sit down, looking out into the audience with a smile.

"How y'all doing?" I ask them. "All right. I'm gonna be singing 'In Color' by Jamey Johnson. So . . . hope y'all enjoy."

I adjust the microphone and then place the guitar strap around my guitar.

Uh—hey, Johnny Cash—you're missing something.

I casually step off the stool and reach for the input jack to plug into my guitar.

"I might need that," I joke.

More chuckles are followed by a wisecrack from a girl, which receives even more laughter. I don't mind. Laughter does indeed soothe your soul. Your nerves too.

I haven't exactly been on a stage many times, getting ready to sing a solo. Sure, I've sung at school and at church, but this is way different.

The chords come easily, but I keep telling myself, *Just get them right. Don't mess it up. Just get to the opening verse.*

"I said, Grandpa, what's this picture here," I start to sing.

Instant applause washes over me. A woman in the crowd says, "Oh my Lord"—and no, it's not my mom! Suddenly I'm off and comfortable and

18

doing something I've always loved to do. Singing a song. Telling a story. Sharing it with the only voice I know—a sound I've heard described in a hundred different ways. "Low" and "deep" and "smooth" and "classic." All I know is that it sounds like me.

It's fall 2009. I'm fifteen, and this is my first "Idol" competition. It's not *American Idol*, however, but "Clayton Idol." You may not have ever heard of it because you may not know about Clayton, North Carolina. Every year, the town ten miles from my hometown of Garner has a harvest festival. "Clayton Idol" is a festival highlight.

My song choice, "In Color," is an ACM and CMA "Song of the Year" by Mercury recording artist Jamey Johnson. The song talks about black-and-white photos belonging to a granddad. I have listened to the song hundreds of times and can actually picture my grandparents in these photos.

By the end of the tune, I'm all in. I'm not singing anymore; it's more like I'm breathing, my soul stirring in these beautiful lyrics that I'm not reciting but rather releasing. Singing can be like pitching; you stand there and slowly and steadily throw a baseball to home plate. The verses and the chords can all be strikes.

I'm confident enough to give the ending a nice resounding twist of melody. The crowd loves it. This time, the whole room is hollering and clapping. Mr. Branch walks over to my side and seems genuinely surprised.

"How many of you watched *America's Got Talent?*" he asks the crowd, and then he says I remind him of the chicken farmer who won the competition recently.

The judges at the front table are asked to share their thoughts. The first judge, a local beauty queen wearing her crown, seems a bit speechless and then says she doesn't have to say anything.

"*That's* how good that was," she tells me.

She's pretty cute.

I feel myself starting to blush.

"You've got that voice," the next judge says. She happens to be Faye Parker of Raleigh, the mother of Clay Aiken of *American Idol* fame.

The third judge, Tina Seldin, a former Raleigh news anchor and a local entertainer herself, speaks with confidence and a strong sense of certainty.

"Scotty, you are what they call 'The Package,' " she begins. "You were born with music in you."

I stand there, nodding and smiling and hoping they all know how much I appreciate these kind compliments.

"Good luck," Tina says. "You will go far."

The words are affirming and fuel up the tank inside of me. Of course, I know there's a big world out there and I'd have to go far—very far—to make my mark on it.

Mom had been telling me to try out for "Clayton Idol" the past month. Or maybe the past year. She gave me a form to fill out and then kept reminding me. One day, she told me she forged my name and sent it in. I joked and told her I was going to sue her, and she just said fifteen-year-olds can't sue their parents.

It's a good thing she signed my name and sent in that form. It turns out I'd eventually win "Clayton Idol."

Little did I know the sparks already inside of me were starting to grow and become brighter. "Clayton Idol" was indeed a fun learning experience, but I had school to focus on and baseball to practice.

You will go far, Scotty.

If only I could have known just how far.

THIS BABY CAN SING

Tina Seldin at "Clayton Idol" was absolutely right about one comment. Not the comment about how far I'd go. Nobody knows how far they'll go in this world. You hope, you pray, and you work hard, but at the end of the day, anything can happen.

She was, however, right about being born with music inside of me. It wasn't just that I loved listening to it; it poured out of me, even at a young age. And it wasn't just that music poured out of me; I loved being watched and also making people laugh and smile.

The story about humming the tune "Bye, Baby Bunting" at the doctor's office at my one-year checkup was true. At the end of that checkup, Mom told my pediatrician, "This baby can sing." She says she looked in my eyes and slowly sang the following three words: "bye, baby Bunting." I stared straight back, bobbing my head, pressing my lips and humming, sending the melody back pitch perfect. The doctor replied with wide eyes, "I don't think I've ever seen that before."

While attending Timber Drive Elementary School, I had a bus driver named Ms. Brenda. Once, on our way to school, she heard me sing, so she encouraged me to keep it up. It got to a

---

While waiting on Scotty during his first dentist visit at age three, I overheard a teenager saying, "Mom, there's a little boy back there in the dentist's chair and he won't tell his name. He just keeps grinning and saying he's the Muffin Man!" I turned and asked, "Hmmm . . . a little boy with big cheeks and blue eyes?" She laughed and said yes. I could only shake my head. "Thought so. He's mine."

JUDY McCREERY

point where Ms. Brenda and the kids would ask me to sing for them, so naturally I'd perform two or three Elvis songs.

One day after I got off the bus, Mom asked me about my musical adventures. "Ms. Brenda told me she just loves the concerts you're giving in the back of the bus. Are you cutting up?"

Mom taught school, both middle and high, so she knew what bus drivers had to deal with. She didn't want me to be one of *those* kids—you know, the kind the drivers would see, let out a sigh, and think twice about opening the door for.

"Ms. Brenda and the kids *want* me to sing. They ask me to sing all the time."

I never did mind. It just seemed natural for my friends and family to encourage me to sing for them. The more they asked, the more comfortable I felt performing, even if it was for one person on the sidewalk or in the school hallway. I didn't walk around feeling like I was carrying some kind of remarkable gift with me; I just enjoyed singing and felt normal doing it anywhere, whether in the children's choir at church or in plays at school.

I actually remember as a kid, after I'd been sick with a cold, slipping into the bathroom, locking the door, and humming and singing a little, just to make sure my voice was okay. It was a legit worry of mine that a cold could mess up my voice. I loved singing too much for that to happen. I wanted to protect it because I knew I *had* to keep singing.

My parents continued to buy me Elvis CDs, which was great because I eventually brought them to gym class. Our PE teacher, Mr. Taylor, said if we brought music to class, we could exercise to it. So of course I brought him some Elvis tunes on my specially mixed CDs. Even as a third grader, I was helping spread my love of the King of Rock and Roll to my classmates.

My interest in music—okay, I'll use that word *obsession* again—grew into a lot of other artists and CDs. One album I played over and over when I was around eight years old was the sound-track of the movie *O Brother, Where Art Thou?* The Grammy Award–winning soundtrack was probably more popular than the movie starring George Clooney. It was produced by the great T Bone Burnett, a famous musician and producer. It had a mixture of country, gospel, blues, blue-grass, and folk music. It opened my eyes and ears to the history and sound of country music. I loved listening to those songs and trying to sound out the notes on my keyboard.

Yeah, I was one of those weird kids.

Even then, I loved music and knew it would always be a part of my life. Yet I couldn't imagine I could do this full-time as a career when I got older. I was just a normal kid from the small town of Garner, North Carolina, who loved to sing and play baseball and hang out with friends. I'm still just a normal guy from Garner who loves to do all of the above. It's awesome to be able to sing in front of huge crowds. And I still get to enjoy baseball as I travel around the country performing. But now I'm a spectator rather than a player. While on the road, I've managed to see some of my favorite Major League Baseball teams. I've also gotten to meet some incredible Major League players such as Josh Beckett, Bryce Harper, Josh Hamilton, Roger Clemens, and Kevin Millar.

I never forget about home, however. Home isn't just a starting point; it's also a place that can ground you and keep you normal, even if your life has suddenly been uprooted and feels anything but.

WATER TOWER TOWN

Garner, North Carolina, could be the setting of a thousand country songs. People living here know what family, faith, and community mean. And food too.

There's something special about North Carolina. Yeah, I know I'm biased, but there's really nothing like our state.

In the western part of our state, you have the gorgeous Appalachian Mountains. These aren't the rocky and rugged kind you find out West, but the rolling sort that seem to pull you in and make you stay. Mix this with cloudy patches that sometimes linger in the valleys and look like gray lakes. This is why the southern part of our mountains are called the Great Smokies. North Carolina's mountains have many wonderful treasures, such as its Cherokee history, the Biltmore estate, awesome ski resorts, and the incredible mile-high swinging bridge on Grandfather Mountain.

On the other side of the state, you have beaches lining the Atlantic Ocean. Places full of tranquil waters, picture-perfect islands, and sea turtles. And, okay, maybe the *occasional* shark. Our beaches are the setting for many movies and love stories, both real and made-up. It's a stark contrast to the Appalachians in the western part of North Carolina.

In between the two, and what I'd like to think

Abraham Lincoln was quoted as saying, "I like to see a man proud of the place in which he lives. I like to see a man live so that his place will be proud of him." Scotty lives this quote daily. I have never seen anyone have so much pride in their home state as Scotty.

NATHAN THOMAS, BASS PLAYER

---

might be the heart of our great state, lies Garner. It's a big small town just ten miles from downtown Raleigh. If I had to sum up Garner in five words, they would be churches, parks, arts, schools, and sports. You will find a church on almost every corner. Garner is not the buckle on the Bible Belt, but close. You could say I was a drug addict growing up—drug to church on Wednesday nights and twice on Sundays. But really, I loved it. I'd see the same kids at church I saw in school or on the ball field, but at church, we were eating, singing, and worshiping. Not a bad way to grow up.

Everyone finds themselves at Lake Benson, a big Garner park, at some point during the year, either watching the North Carolina Symphony and the fireworks on July 3 or walking one of the paved paths. Kids are either playing baseball at GBI (Garner Baseball, Inc.), dancing at Christy's DancExplosion, or auditioning for plays at the Garner Performing Arts Center. The high school Blue Crew fills the stands at Friday night football games in the fall, while the gym is full for winter basketball games and the baseball field bleachers are crowded in the spring. As a side note, I like to remind my friends who went to local rival high schools that Garner was the last Wake County school to win a football state championship. We also won the 4A basketball state championship in 2015.

Those baseball fields are something I know quite well. Growing up in Garner, I did love to sing. But I think I might have loved playing baseball even more.

Music might be in my soul, but baseball's in my blood.

DAD

My dad, Mike, has played baseball his whole life. That's where I got my love and passion for it.

He has lots of awesome traits. I've tried to pick up a few of those over the years. One of those is the ability to pitch.

Dad was born in Puerto Rico, but grew up in Maine. He was a great pitcher in high school. Actually, he was pretty good in all sports, and he still golfs and plays baseball. He eventually moved to North Carolina to attend college and to get away from the cold. He pitched and golfed while attending a junior college. It was in North Carolina that he met this beautiful woman named Judy and fell in love with her. My dad later graduated from NC State. My mom, however, graduated from UNC-Chapel Hill. In North Carolina, we call that a mixed marriage, but Mom and Dad have made it work for thirty years.

For those of you wondering which side of the fence I'm on, I am and will forever be a part of the NC State Wolfpack. I was lucky enough to attend NC State after graduating from Garner High. My parents were married in 1986 while my dad was finishing his degree. They settled in Garner, not too far from NC State's campus. In 1990, they welcomed a charming, kind, and sweet child into their family. No, I'm not talking about myself. I'm referring to my sister, Ashley. When Ash was born, my father began working for Schneider Electric, known years ago as Square D. My mother, a teacher, eventually went into real estate sales and marketing.

As I grew up in Garner, it was natural for Dad to instill his love of baseball in me. The scene of father and son playing catch was seen many times in our yard. Dad also coached my baseball teams when I was younger.

I continued to learn and become better at the sport, eventually pitching for Garner High. As a senior, even after missing most of my junior year due to *Idol*, I finished the year with a 0.88 ERA and struck out fifty batters. Come on—let me brag a little. Singers don't get to have stats like those.

I absolutely loved pitching and loved to tell folks that not only was my dad a great pitcher, but I was even related to the famous MLB pitcher from North Carolina, Jim "Catfish" Hunter. Just so happens, the late, great Catfish Hunter of Oakland Athletics and New York Yankees fame hailed from Hertford in Perquimans County,

North Carolina. Well, my great-granddad was also a "Hunter" from Perquimans County. I've never been able to find a family link, but a guy can dream, right? I even said in an on-camera interview at the MLB Fan Cave in New York City I was related to Catfish. My mom was nearby and almost had a stroke, reminding me afterward that we had no proof. She felt so bad about it that she mailed a package of Scotty goodies to Catfish's widow, Helen Hunter, with an explanation of why I said what I did, just in case she had heard about my comment.

So while I continued to play baseball, I still had this music thing going on. And a crazy dream in my head too.

MAKING THE LADIES CRY

In my sophomore year of high school, I tried my hand in a school play while also playing baseball. My classmates asked me to try out for the role of Conrad Birdie in the play *Bye Bye Birdie*. It's really a fictionalized story of Elvis Presley getting drafted into the army. The name Conrad Birdie, however, is a play on Conway Twitty's name. Twitty was a popular singer when the musical first came out in 1963. There's some debate over whether the whole musical was about him, but to me, I saw Elvis in Conrad Birdie, so naturally it was the perfect fit for me. It was such a blast singing songs like "A Lot of Livin' to Do" and "One Last Kiss" in front of a packed theater. Can anybody say *foreshadowing?*

But man, those were two stressful weeks. Play practice was before *and* after school, but baseball season had started and I didn't want to lose my spot on the team. I'd dart out of play practice and head to baseball practice, usually getting there late. My baseball coach wasn't thrilled. When the play finally ended, Coach Goffena jokingly asked, "What's next, McCreery? *Idol?*"

There are just so many random events that eventually landed me on that TV show. For a few years, my mom owned a salon in nearby Clayton. She hired an employee named Shirley, who also worked for the Clayton Chamber of Commerce. One afternoon, Mom noticed Shirley was having a bad day, so she told me to grab my guitar from the back of her Jeep and sing a song for Shirley.

"No way! I don't randomly sing in front of people like that," I said.

But Mom kept begging me. So when the customers left, I got my guitar and sang "Long Black Train" by Josh Turner.

Shirley started to cry. It was a pretty surreal feeling, singing and then seeing tears on someone else's face. Afterward, Shirley encouraged me to sign up for the talent show she was coordinating—"Clayton Idol."

It's hard to say no to a woman in tears.

WHAT IF?

"There's an audition coming up in Nashville on July 17."

I'm in the kitchen, and Mom is standing by her laptop, giving me information on the first of two upcoming *American Idol* auditions. All I can do is stand there and give her a look. Not the "you're crazy" look or the "I'm not going to waste my time doing that" look.

This look has to be somewhat unusual, because I'm feeling a mix of a lot of different things.

There's no way I'd get the golden ticket, but it would be a cool thing to do.

But wouldn't that be awesome if I did?

What would the judges say?

They might hate me. . . . They might love me.

These thoughts all become moot points when I realize the date of the Nashville audition is the same time as my annual summer church retreat.

"Uh-oh," I tell her. "No way. I'm not missing Camp Caswell with all my buds just to go get cut from a TV show."

We've discussed the idea of auditioning for *Idol*, so the conversation isn't coming out of nowhere. After I won "Clayton Idol" at the age of fifteen, the seeds had been planted. I mean—I'd won $75 in the talent show. But more importantly, the crowd's reaction had genuinely surprised me.

Sure, I won the talent show, but the crowd *liked* me. A very small part of me asked, "Can I actually do this?" It made me want to go to more concerts and see the country music world up close. Over the next year, I attended every country concert within a couple hours' drive of Raleigh. I saw George Strait, Reba McEntire, Trace Adkins, Toby Keith, Emmylou Harris, Montgomery Gentry, Josh Turner, Jamey Johnson, Chris Young, and Ronnie Milsap. Of course, Garth wasn't touring then, but I bought his concert DVD and sat for hours on my living room floor, watching him entertain thousands and even crowd surf in the audience.

After winning "Clayton Idol," I had continued to look for other places to perform. I got some great experience at a local community college showcase, as well as singing at nearby restaurants and our local performing arts center. I even had the opportunity to open for bluegrass performers Dale Ann Bradley and Lorraine Jordan, and for a country musician, Jason Michael Carroll.

One night after singing for a church dinner in downtown Raleigh, the group took up a good ole Southern love offering, which they bestowed upon me in a Ziploc bag as I got ready to leave. I was surprised, but I casually told them thanks and then proceeded to tear it open once I was alone in the parking lot. The bag was a few pennies shy of one hundred dollars.

Holy smokes, I thought.

I immediately felt guilty because my sister, Ash, was waiting tables that night at her job. I knew Ash wouldn't make this much money in a whole weekend—and I had made it in thirty minutes.

Hmmmm. I think I'm on to something.

The seeds had been planted.

Our family had always tuned in to *Idol.* Season 9 was no different. This was Simon Cowell's last season, and Lee DeWyze won. Notable singers that season included Crystal Bowersox, Casey James, and Aaron Kelly.

There was something about watching that season. Maybe it was because I had that bug from "Clayton Idol." Maybe it was all those concerts I'd attended. Or because I was getting older. But for whatever reason, I watched with a little more interest. When the finale arrived, I remember this thought: *Why can't I do that?*

It wasn't a cocky thought, nor did it have anything to do with the talented singers that year. It was more of a "that might be pretty cool" kind of thing. Ryan Seacrest gave the places and dates for tryouts for next year's show. Moments later, we were behind the computer but still thinking it wasn't going to happen.

Oh well. It was fun to think about.

"There's an audition in Milwaukee," Mom says as she looks at the computer before I head out of the kitchen. "July 21."

It's after the church retreat, so the date works. "We could use your dad's frequent flyer miles to make the trip," she says. "We don't have to tell anybody about the audition. It'd just be fun to see what happens."

I stand there smiling. It's a crazy thought, but a fun one too.

A COUPLE OF FAILURES

There's a story about a teenager who went to an audition for a band one day. He told them he drove a truck for a living. After the audition ended, the young man was told he better stick to his day job since he was never going to make it as a singer.

Just another failed audition. Happens all the time.

I heard another story about a young man who mustered up the courage to enter a famous recording studio in the hope of getting a record contract. After he sang several gospel songs, it's rumored the studio head told him to go out and sin a little and come back with a song the man could go out and sell.

Just one more failed dream. Hardly worth mentioning.

Except this didn't stop Elvis Presley or Johnny Cash from continuing to pursue their dreams.

Eddie Bond was a singer already well-known on the Memphis music scene when a young and nervous Elvis came into the Hi-Hat Club in May 1954 to audition as a singer with his group. The young Elvis did drive a truck for Crown Electric, and Eddie was convinced he certainly didn't have a future.

As for Johnny Cash, he was already playing guitar and learning the craft when he visited the famous Sun Records studio in 1954 with a goal of being offered a contract. The songs he sang didn't impress producer Sam Phillips, who actually did tell Johnny to go out and get a little more grit under his fingernails if he wanted to make a record.

They were just simple auditions, right? And these two failed. And, of course, they went on to both have pretty good careers, right?

My worst thought about trying out for *American Idol* wasn't that I would be cut right away. The worst that could happen would be working hard to make it through the early rounds, only to be cut in a later round.

For me, it was a simple scenario: get cut right away or go to Hollywood and win the whole thing.

I'm not the type to ever back down, regardless of how nice and friendly a guy I may seem to be. I'm pretty competitive. I may come off as a laid-back guy, but I got a little fire on the inside. Just when you think you've got me figured out, I'll throw you a curveball.

My last baseball game before leaving for *Idol* demonstrated that. It was a hot, steamy July night. We were playing rival Fuquay on their home field. I had played the entire game and was pitching a shutout. I was soaking wet but loving every minute of it. My signature pitch was a slider-curveball combination I called "the slurve." It was effective that night. But even more effective were my teammates behind me. You can only pitch a shutout if the guys on the field are backing you up.

In the sixth inning, things got tense. I gave up back-to-back hits. There were runners on second and third with no outs. Coach Pake walked out to the mound to pull me.

"I'm finishing this," I told him. "I'm not giving up the ball. I got this."

After a few moments of talking it out, the coach decided to let me stay on the mound. I struck out the next six batters to win the game.

I already knew something then, but I believed it even more after that game: It's not about stepping out and making a leap of faith; it's about finishing strong and knowing you've not held anything back.

WHY NOT?

It's the summer of 2010. The idea of auditioning for *American Idol* is up in the air. And I'm

37

standing here thinking about the time Elvis and Johnny auditioned.

Why are you comparing yourself to these guys? a doubting Thomas voice whispers in my head.

Another voice answers. *They were both just two young, inexperienced singers trying to follow a dream. They weren't legends stepping into those studios.*

I realize something. The legend doesn't begin when you first step into that studio; it starts by being yourself and giving it a shot and letting the rest of the world decide the sort of story they want to tell about you.

I remember the quote by the late NC State basketball coach Jim Valvano: "Every single day in every walk of life, ordinary people do extraordinary things."

I think of that last baseball game I pitched— and then I know.

I know without a doubt I'm going to step up to the mound and give it my all.

And maybe, just maybe, I'll still be around in the last inning.

Chapter Two

A Little Field Trip

The soulful voice belts out an a capella version of "I Heard It Through the Grapevine" joined by the thousands surrounding him in the Bradley Center, Milwaukee's indoor arena. Soon we're all invited to stand up and sing "My Girl." Even though we're in the nosebleed section, we still recognize the singer leading our group from a past *Idol* season.

Before he leaves the arena, he looks out at the crowd and makes the following declaration: "The next American Idol is going to come from these auditions in my hometown—Milwaukee, Wisconsin!"

We all erupt and applaud the third-place finalist on Season 8 of *American Idol*. Little do any of us truly realize Danny Gokey will be right.

Milwaukee is indeed the starting point for this wild adventure.

WAY OVER MY HEAD

We've been up since 5:00 a.m., watching the audition process get started at the Bradley Center. There've been numerous welcomes, including a very enthusiastic one from Ryan Seacrest himself. He reminds us that every year the contest starts like this—with people sitting in an arena, looking down on the main floor. Hoping and believing. Weeks will pass, and they'll turn into months—and a winner will eventually be crowned.

Ryan even asks the inevitable question: "Is the next *American Idol* winner here in Milwaukee?"

I raise my hand. Of course, so do the thousands of other hopefuls in the Bradley Center.

"Are you going to take the title?"

More cheers. Ryan silences the crowd and tells everybody the hard, cold, brutal truth.

"You get one shot."

Mom, Dad, and I flew to Milwaukee without telling a single soul. We didn't even tell my sister. She's working this summer as a counselor at the NC Baptist Assembly's Camp Caswell on the coast at Oak Island—the same camp I didn't want to miss by attending the Nashville audition. We didn't tell Ashley or anyone else simply because we figured they'd laugh or roll their eyes, thinking we're crazy. Maybe we are.

We all figure this will be a fun trip we'll be able to talk about one day. We'll sit around during a family meal and say, "Hey, remember that time we went up to Wisconsin to try out for *Idol*?"

It is July, so it's not like I had to skip school. Dad racked up enough frequent flyer miles and hotel points last year, so the trip is practically free. Just a fun family outing.

I don't think we'll ever forget some of the people who auditioned. Anybody who's seen the show knows for some, the tryouts suddenly become synonymous with Halloween. We've seen the Riddler from *Batman*, as well as a woman dressed as a beer can wearing a cheesehead. Several clowns, of course—some just behaving like clowns, but also literal clowns completely decked out.

The floor is lined with a dozen tables where judges sit to listen to auditions. These are judges you don't see on the show. They may be involved with show production or the record label. Black curtains separate the tables, forming what looks like an oversized starting gate at a horse race. Small groups are called into each numbered section to sing for however long the judges will let them.

"I definitely don't want to go to table 3," I tell my folks.

We've been watching, listening to, and studying this circus for the last few hours. The groups of performers are led like lambs to the . . . I mean, they will be led by arena security to the tables where they'll get their chance to sing. Very few are given golden tickets, the official invitations to come back and continue auditions. We're all wearing the wristbands we were given the day

41

before. Once you're done, either you're directed backstage with a golden ticket in hand or you're directed to the doors where someone will be kind enough to cut off your wristband and politely bid you a nice rest of your life. Or something like that.

You pretty much have to stay in the same arena seat all day. The girl seated next to me is a few years older than me and is sitting next to her dad. She's covered in tattoos, and she's not wearing any deodorant. It's July, and it's hot . . . We strike up a conversation, and she tells me how excited she is to see Randy Jackson, Jennifer Lopez, and Steven Tyler. I hate to burst her bubble, but I tell her those judges aren't here today.

"If you make it through today, you'll be able to see the big judges on a different day," I tell her.

She suddenly looks seriously bummed. Not only that, I don't even think she believes me.

I decide I really need some fresh air and a fresh smell, plus I'm a little hungry. I get out of my seat to find something to eat. In the hallways of the arena, a variety of young people are standing and rehearsing and talking. A few are even sleeping. A crowd has formed around a pair of singers playing the guitar and sounding like they're onstage at the Grand Ole Opry.

These guys are good. Like, really good.

Another young woman I pass is singing to a group, and she looks like she's already been on the show. She's gotta be a semiprofessional or at least doing some gigs somewhere.

My stomach that had just been rumbling a short while ago now doesn't feel so hungry. I walk around for a few more minutes before heading back to my seat. I scan the arena before sitting down. Mom's getting her exercise walking around the building, so it's just my dad sitting next to me.

"What am I doing here?" I ask him as I let out a sigh. "I'm in way over my head."

"Just do your best, and we'll see what happens."

Dad sounds just like he has any other time I've had to do something, whether it's pitching in a game or dealing with some kind of problem. There's no worry in his tone, nor is there a hint of questioning why we came.

It gives me a burst of confidence. Staring down at the cattle call on the floor below, I know I'm going to need it.

MY BIG SIS

The confidence that many have seen in me has come from different sources. One huge source has been Ashley, my older sister. She's the best sister a guy could possibly ask for.

Ashley is three and half years older than me, making it easy for us to get along and grow close since there wasn't much sibling rivalry. She's a source of constant encouragement and love and also demonstrates how to overcome obstacles.

My big sister grew up being very shy. This didn't stop her, however, from trying to make friends and pursuing things that interested her. She made good grades, but they came because she worked super hard. She was the kid who started projects early and kept a neat desk. I didn't get that gene. Sports were a constant part of Ashley's life, just like they were in mine. She might not have been the star of the team, but she often won awards like the sportsmanship award or was made a co-captain of a team. I witnessed a special quality in Ashley that I try to imitate to this day—persistence.

The thing that meant the most to me, however, wasn't her example of putting herself out there all the time; it was her encouragement and acceptance of her little brother. I mean, what sort of high school girl lets her middle school brother hang out with her at her high school games? Ashley *liked* me, and while this might sound a bit silly, it meant the world to me.

It still does.

Now, I have to admit I haven't always been the best brother. Like the time I filled up her bathtub and let a turtle take a swim. Let's just say Ashley has some lungs. Then there was the time she almost jumped from our second floor. I was standing outside her bedroom door, and I heard her calling Dad on her cell phone as she opened her window. She said she was gonna jump. I kinda forgot to tell her I was home early from school. I guess cocking my pellet gun outside her door made her think there was an intruder? Maybe?

And then there was "the Clapper." One year for Christmas, my mom had gotten a clapper as a gag gift—you know, those devices you plug your lamp into and then you clap it on and off. Well, I was about eight or nine. I just *had* to have the clapper. For quite a few nights, I'd hear Ash down the hall, yelling, "Scotty, cut it out!"

THIRTY SECONDS

Even though Ashley isn't in the Bradley Center, I still feel like she's on the sideline cheering me on. When I get called and finally stand in front of a table with a judge who points at me to sing, I don't see my life flash before my eyes. I don't think about all those hours practicing guitar or singing in chorus class. I just let it happen. And yes, I can hear Ash saying in the background, "Come on, Scotty! You got this!"

It just feels good to stand, since my rear end was falling asleep sitting on the hard seat in the arena. And this thought keeps floating through my head.

I'd rather be down here on the main floor than up in the stands.

Earlier, when the security guard called our

section to walk down to the main floor, I joked with him and asked if he could get our group a female judge. We noticed that more women than men are handing out golden tickets. The guard laughed and said he'd see what he could do. Thankfully, I'm now standing in front of a pretty, ginger-haired woman who is welcoming us with smiles. After the other three singers in my group finish up, she looks my way.

"So what are you going to sing?" she asks me.

" 'Your Man' by Josh Turner."

Just a few days earlier, I met Josh at a meet and greet at the Alabama Theatre in Myrtle Beach. I doubt he would remember the brief meeting, but getting a chance to shake his hand still stands out. I told him I was going to an *Idol* audition in Milwaukee in a few days and was planning to sing one of his songs.

"That's far, far away," Josh told me.

I assumed he was talking about Wisconsin, but then again, maybe he was referring to getting on the show and trying to win it.

But first things first. I've been here at the Bradley Center in Milwaukee since 5:00 a.m. I'm finally in front of a judge. This next minute could change my life. Well, maybe.

Time to lock them doors and turn the lights down low.

I know the song inside and out. I also know I'll have about thirty seconds to share it. I take a deep breath, clear my throat, and step up to the plate.

"Baby lock them doors . . ."

She doesn't stop me as quickly as she stopped the others in my group. My mind is racing. I can tell she's thinking. If she thought I stunk, she would have stopped me by now. After I finish the whole chorus of "Your Man," she asks me to sing another song.

Another song is good! It's a good sign when they ask you to sing something else!

Still, I know the reality with country music. Some folks just don't get it. And sure enough, this judge informs me this isn't *Nashville Star*. She asks if I can sing something besides country. I'm armed and ready. I go with Sinatra.

"Some day, when I'm awfully low . . ."

It's nice to be singing "The Way You Look Tonight" to a lady. Just sayin'. But even after I

47

muster up as much charm as I can for the Sinatra classic, she still isn't sold.

Still no golden ticket.

"Can you sing something else?"

It's like déjà vu. Didn't she just ask me this?

"Sure, but it's gonna be a country song," I say.

Flashback to "Clayton Idol." She's getting ready to hear Jamey Johnson's "In Color."

Just like in 2009, Jamey comes through for me again. The judge pulls out a golden ticket but doesn't hand it over until she gives me a little feedback, as well as a little homework.

"Look," the judge says, "I'm gonna put you through, but you need to learn a pop song for the next round tomorrow."

"Sure thing," I say as I shake her hand.

She asks for a quick picture before she lets me walk away. Little do I realize it will be the first of many pictures taken on this journey.

My folks rush down from the stands and meet me on the main floor. My dad is massaging his upper arm, which my mom has been grabbing the past five minutes as she watched this drama unfold. Their smiles are priceless.

SIGN ON THE DOTTED LINE

Remember the moment in *Willy Wonka & the Chocolate Factory* when the kids are about to step foot into the factory? Willy Wonka asks them to step up to a platform, and then he pulls back a curtain to reveal a massive ten-foot-tall contract on the wall with text that starts big on the top and gets smaller and smaller until it practically vanishes.

"Violet, you first," Willy Wonka says. "Sign here."

Her father quickly steps in, telling Wonka, "I don't sign anything without my lawyer."

Another father says the same thing. Willy Wonka just grins.

"Then you don't go in," he says. "Rules of the house."

Veruca Salt, the spoiled girl in the group, pushes her father away and grabs the pen from Wonka.

I can't help but think of that scene as we step into a room in the arena where we're given some forms to fill out. One is a basic info sheet. Then a few other pieces of paper.

Mom starts looking through them, having experience with detailed contracts from working in real estate.

"I'm not signing this," she says.

Since I'm just sixteen and still a minor—a constant reminder that will start and won't end until the finale of the show—my parents have to put their signatures on the paperwork.

Dad and I look at her like she's crazy.

"Just sign it," I tell her.

We know others are waiting to get in here who are more than willing to sign papers like these if we don't.

WE'VE GOT A SECRET

"So the next round of auditions will be tomorrow," a producer tells us.

The realities of life suddenly sink in. We have three plane tickets booked to fly back to North Carolina tomorrow. Our home, jobs, and lives are back in Garner. Now we need to rearrange some things. Thanks to Dad and the fine folks at Delta, he manages to change the flights. It sure helps to have a gazillion air miles racked up.

When we finally get outside the arena, shadows have fallen over Milwaukee. We've been up fourteen hours, and it's now dusk.

"We need to call Ash," Mom says as she gets her phone and begins to dial.

All of us are feeling rotten that Ashley doesn't know we're five states away. Since we have to stay another day, we decide we need to come clean and tell her we took a little field trip.

But she can't tell a soul.

Mom puts her on speaker so we can all hear her reaction.

"Ash, are you by yourself?" Mom asks. "You're not around any campers or the other counselors, are you?"

"Yeah, I'm by myself. What's up?" she asks.

"We have something to tell you. We're in Milwaukee."

"What?"

"At the *American Idol* auditions."

"WHAT?"

"And Scotty made it through the first round."

The sound of Ashley's screams are all we can hear. Hopefully nobody can hear her and ask what's going on.

"Don't tell a soul," Mom says. "We just signed confidentiality forms."

This will be another constant theme for the next few months—not telling anyone. The show keeps a tight lid on news about each upcoming season in order to make the biggest impact once it's announced. So we *have* to keep quiet. And it's sure tougher than it may sound.

Now our whole family of four knows. I think about my relatives and friends. About the guys on my baseball team and the coach.

Wouldn't it be crazy if I actually got on the show?

All of them—heck, the whole town of Garner— would go nuts. It would be Ashley's reaction times 28,000.

It'd sure be pretty cool.

51

BAD ROMANCE

"I need a pop song," I tell my parents that night while dining at Applebee's in downtown Milwaukee.

One of the last things the friendly, ginger-haired judge told me was to learn some other songs. The producer's name is Katie. She's the one who really discovered me.

I know at tomorrow's round I need to show I'm a diverse singer who can stretch myself, but it's still encouraging to be reminded of this by Katie. I can't just rely on the songs I'm most comfortable with.

It's not that I don't know other songs, like what's current on the radio or the kind of music my friends like. I've just always been that sort of kid who liked listening to country—and not just current country artists like Lady Antebellum and Jason Aldean, but also old-school tunes from Conway Twitty, Merle Haggard, and Ronnie Milsap.

"What about 'Slow Dancing in a Burning Room'?" Mom suggests.

I had sung the John Mayer song at the end-of-the-year choral event at school.

"You killed it," Dad reminds me.

It's a silky, brooding song, and a good tune for my voice. The next day arrives, and I'm auditioning for higher-level judges. I end up doing both the Josh Turner and the John Mayer songs, and they go well. But all of us contestants had been asked to learn a popular song on the radio and told we *may* have to sing it.

"Did you learn that Lady Gaga song?" these new judges ask me after I perform my first two songs.

"Yeah," I say.

I've been dreading this.

"Go ahead," they say.

I start to sing "Bad Romance"—the song everybody in America knows. By the time I'm singing "rah rah ah-ah-ah," I have to stop.

"This is not on my country station back home," I tell them.

The producers burst out in laughter.

"We know. We just wanted to hear you sing it," they tell me. "You're through to the next round."

So it's day two in Milwaukee. Yesterday was the cattle call. I've just made it through round 2, and now it's the third round of auditions. I'm in front of the executive producers of the show and the recording company execs. I sing "Your Man," "The Way You Look Tonight," and "Slow Dancing in a Burning Room." Then I do Jamey Johnson's "In Color." When I finish, the guy from the label compliments me but asks a question. "Scotty, you sound good, but I'm confused. Are you country, or are you pop?"

I can only smile. "Man, I was raised on corn-bread and sweet tea. I'm a country singer."

That seems to be what they want to hear. Then they tell me what I want to hear—that I'll be back for the big audition in front of the main judges, the auditions they show on television, the ones the viewers always see first. It's only two and a half months away.

Yeah. Only seventy-five days or so.

On the flight home that night, my parents are still in shock. I overhear my dad asking my mom a question.

"How far do you think he can go?"

"Based on the reaction he got the last two days, maybe all the way," she says.

MOM

My mom, Judy, she's always been a believer. And she's always believed being a parent is one of God's greatest blessings. She and her mom—my grandma Janet—were both teachers. They each felt all kids have unique gifts and it's a parent's responsibility to recognize those gifts and nurture them. That's why she took me to my first guitar lessons and why she forged my name on that talent show form. That's why even now she hounds me until I get my vocal cords scoped at Duke Voice Care each year and even has her pharmacist girlfriend surprise me with a flu shot every fall. She's also the one who spent a solid year supervising my first house being built on the coast and later found me a fixer-upper ski condo in the mountains. Nothing too fancy, but my first investments. And she insists I take time off to recharge my batteries at these places. She insists folks on my team use these places too. She likes to say she's my property manager.

Mom only spanked me once, and boy, does she remember it. She says I was around three. When she went for my bottom, I was holding a toy airplane fighter jet in my hand—of course, trying to cover my rear. Well, when she took a whack, the point of the jet went right into her palm. We had to drive to the doctor's office, where he popped some of that neat crazy glue into the wound. She said she felt like God was saying, "Hands off the kids," after that episode.

It wasn't my parents' style to spank or hit anyway. They could accomplish a lot with the big eyes and raising their voices a bit. They would also dangle carrots instead of taking things away. Instead of "you're gonna lose this if your grades are bad," it was more "you'll earn this" or "you'll be able to do this," if we did our best.

Mom "redshirted" me in preschool. Yeah, can you believe that? My birthday made the school cutoff date by a week. But after teaching middle school for years and being tortured by immature seventh grade boys, she knew she'd never let her own son be the baby in the class.

"Girls can pull off being the youngest in a classroom," she would say. "Boys—not so much."

"Mentally, socially, physically, it gives a child an advantage to be one of the oldest in his or her class," she would preach. "They'll experience more success, which will create more confidence."

Well, that was her theory, anyway.

Even at the age of five, however, I knew what was going on and wasn't too happy. I get her back sometimes by telling others I flunked preschool, which drives her wild.

Many have called me an old soul. Maybe it started way back in kindergarten.

THE JUDGES

It's October, and I'm back in Milwaukee. It's quite a bit chillier than when I was here in July. Our instructions were to wear the exact outfit we wore in July, which means flip-flops for me. And yes, it gives Ryan Seacrest something to comment on as I'm waiting to see the judges. I'm a nervous wreck, and the camera guys are panning to my feet.

I'll be seventeen a week from now. Sure, I'm young, but that doesn't mean I'm not prepared for today. Preparation is more than strengthening your vocal cords and practicing lyrics; it also means being sharp and coming armed with knowledge. You have to be ready for any question they might toss at you, prepared to meet anybody, and set to sing any song they might suggest.

While deciding on songs for the big audition, I was also doing my homework on the judges. I saw Randy had produced an album for one of my favorite artists, Travis Tritt. It was then I decided to learn a Tritt song for the audition. I'd found a connection with the Dawg.

So here are a few things I know about the three judges I'm about to meet. Things that not everybody at home or even auditioning might be aware of.

Randy Jackson isn't just the fun-loving judge full of memorable catchphrases and phrases like "dawg" and "yo" and "in it to win it." The reason he was chosen as one of the original judges on *American Idol* was his incredible musical legacy. One of the most successful session bassists ever, Randy was hired to play bass for some of music's top artists. The list of people he's played with includes

- Bruce Springsteen
- Bob Dylan
- Billy Joel
- Aretha Franklin
- Stevie Nicks
- Roger Waters
- Bon Jovi

Quite some list.

Randy played bass for the megaband Journey in 1986 on their *Raised on Radio* album and toured with them for a couple years. He's run his own label and produced many albums.

Credibility? Few have it like Randy Jackson does.

Then there's Jennifer Lopez. Or as everyone knows her, the incomparable J.Lo.

Born in New York to Puerto Rican parents, she knew at a young age she wanted to be an entertainer. She's been singing and dancing her whole life. She began lessons at age five. She actually danced behind New Kids on the Block at the American Music Awards when she was twenty-one years old. A big break came when she got the starring role in the movie *Selena.* She became the first actress to have a number one movie at the same time her album was number one on the charts.

She loves the incredible performers like Tina Turner, Michael Jackson, James Brown, Madonna, and Janet Jackson. Obviously, you can see their influence on her. A true triple threat, she's the star who can sing, act, and dance.

Then there's Steven Tyler. Like, seriously? I'm about to walk in front of Steven Tyler.

If you're a country soul and have never fully listened to Aerosmith, let me suggest you put the book down (just for a few moments) to find the loudest speakers around and crank up "Sweet Emotion." The opening guitar and bass seem to crawl all over you as the anticipation begins before the drums and voices start. And then, boom. It's off. It explodes. Rock at its finest.

There's "Walk This Way"—Aerosmith's famous song later covered by the rap group Run-D.M.C. Musical genres all merge and morph together these days, but back then, they were pretty solid camps. Aerosmith broke new ground. Who knows? Maybe Steven Tyler would keep it up and try his hand at country one day . . .

Then listen to *Big Ones*, as their "greatest hits" album is called, which includes "Rag Doll," "Dude (Looks Like a Lady)," "Janie's Got a Gun," and "The Other Side." They've written some pretty amazing tunes! My favorite might be "Dream On"—their classic ballad from the seventies. The vocals. *The vocals.*

I've done my homework on the three people sitting in front of me. It's always good to do your homework and be prepared.

So, yeah, I'm sixteen and about to sing in front of these three. All legends in pop, R&B, and classic rock.

Good thing I'm singin' country.

Sarcasm comes in handy to battle the nerves.

THE BIG AUDITION

Many people will end up seeing that first audition and getting their first look at Scotty McCreery. I'm the one who says I'm an all-American kid. They ask my age, and then Jennifer makes a remark about me having such a low voice at my age. The mind-blown part of me is thinking, *I can't believe I'm hearing these comments* and *Look how beautiful she is in person!*

The song I'm about to sing was only officially cleared by the show for rights a few moments ago. The producers told me earlier the song had to be cleared in order to put the audition on television. If it's not cleared, it doesn't mean you won't make it through, but America might not see you sing it. I told them it didn't matter. "Your Man" is my choice. Thankfully, the song gets cleared shortly before my audition on that cold October day in Milwaukee.

I don't change anything I've done. I simply start singing like I always have. By the time I'm singing the second line, I'm staring straight at Jennifer.

"Well, I've been thinking about this all day long."

She gives me maybe one of the best grins I'll ever see in my life, and it doesn't go away. Even after I stop singing.

I know her expression is a good thing, but I'm

not so sure about the laughter that follows. I once told myself as a kid that if I ever made it on *American Idol* and got laughed at by the judges, I'd just walk out. I'd keep my dignity and just step out of the room. But Jennifer puts any fears at rest right away.

"You make me smile," she proclaims.

I'm done. Thank you very much. Scotty McCreery, winner of the Jennifer Lopez Adoration Contest.

They ask me to sing another song to show my range, so I choose that song I love by Travis Tritt. I give a shout-out to Randy for producing an album with him.

Homework, baby.

"Put Some Drive in Your Country" is the song that produces perhaps the best line ever uttered

---

It amazes me that in 2011, I sat, awed, watching Scotty on *Idol*. With the show over, I felt post-show depression and needed to find ways to support this young man in his career. So this grandma got on the web, joined Twitter, joined fan bases, voted on polls, bought music, gifted music, and told everyone she met about Scotty!!! Still doing this every day!!

DOT BANNER,
McCREERIAN FROM FLORIDA

---

on the show. It comes from Steven Tyler, and he shares it immediately after I finish.

"Well, hellfire, save matches, **** a duck, and see what hatches."

Instant insanity spills over onto the set. Randy Jackson is standing in disbelief. Everybody, including the guys operating the cameras and microphones, are laughing hysterically. All the while, I'm just smiling and staying cool. I didn't know what to think.

"That's amazing," Steven says. "That's beautiful."

"I can see a real artist there," Jennifer says.

"I love it. I love it," Randy adds.

Hey, they're talking about me.

With three resounding yeses, they tell me I'm off to Hollywood. I ask if I can shake their hands. I thank them. It's the right thing to do.

This time, Ashley is there, waiting in the hall-way along with my parents to see the golden ticket I hide at first. It's an incredible moment. It's actually tough to take it all in because of the joy and the surprise and the thrill pumping inside of me.

It stays there. For . . .

Well, actually, I don't think it's ever left.

ONE SHOT

I was indeed raised on country classics, just like the Travis Tritt song says. There's no way to hide that. My voice and my style and my everything reveal this. I already know the box I'm going to be put into, and that's fine. I love that box.

Nobody can ever change your voice, not once you've discovered it. The thing is—life's all about figuring out when and how to use it.

And I'm not talking about your literal voice; I'm talking about *you*.

I will later see a comment that was made after I left the audition. A visibly animated Jennifer Lopez shakes her head and keeps smiling.

"With the right songs . . . We discovered him."

The right songs indeed. There's going to be a lot more to sing before this is over. Lots more.

I think back to the last thing Ryan Seacrest told us in the Bradley Center in Milwaukee: "You Get. One. Shot to make the first impression. Don't hold anything back. This is for the big leagues. This is for the big time. This will . . . Change . . . Your . . . Life."

Yeah.

I suddenly realize Ryan is absolutely right.

Chapter Three

The Man I Want to Be

The hallway of the hotel feels too quiet and too long. It's the middle of the night, and I should be exhausted and ready to sleep. I send a quick text to my guys back home. I tell them, "I'm getting cut; see y'all soon." I walk to my room and only feel regret. Echoes of doubt follow my footsteps.

I should've done something.

Sure, what's done is done. I get that. And yeah, this is a competition, but still.

I know I could've done more earlier tonight. I didn't.

This is what compromise looks like, and it sure ain't pretty.

I can't start out like this. It's just not right.

Some people say winning is everything. I'm really competitive, so I get it. If you're around me when my Wolfpack is playing, watch out. But life's bigger than that. We're supposed to be better than that too. There are things more important than winning.

Nobody should let someone else struggle, whether it's a neighbor you know or a kid you meet in a singing competition.

But I just went ahead and let it happen.

The memory of a Hank Williams Jr. song reminds me a country boy can survive. Even in Hollywood. Even after getting this far and making a mistake. I just have to man up and move on.

Lord, give me strength.

There's always tomorrow. Which, I guess, technically, is today.

JACEE BADEAUX

Jacee Badeaux was the first to accept me into his group, so I should've been the first to say he couldn't leave it. I'm still not exactly sure how I got to this moment in the first place.

The first two days of Hollywood Week at the Pasadena Civic Center find the judges eliminating about half of the singers. This season is different because twice the number of contestants have been given a golden ticket to Hollywood. I don't need to be a math genius to know it'll be twice as easy to be sent home.

If you've never seen *Idol*, here's a quick overview of what happens during Hollywood Week. Groups of ten are sent onto the stage during those first couple of days. We are individually given a chance to sing a capella and given no feedback. We each have one shot—do-or-die, sudden death . . . I'm starting to sound like an ESPN commentator. But it's true. Just like you see on the shows, folks in the group are told to step forward or back, and boom—your fate is sealed. Some will have all the right pieces. Some are going to put forth a great effort. But in a game of inches, it's going to be blood, sweat . . .

Well, okay, sports clichés aside, there may not be any blood and comparatively little sweat, but there *are* tears. On the stage and off.

I stuck to the song I felt I knew the best. The contestants around me had never heard me sing, so my rendition of "Your Man" gets a nice round of applause and expressions of surprise. Since I get through my audition on the first day, I have time to find a few others willing to sing with me in the much-feared upcoming group round. We had a great group—a couple guys and some pretty girls. Then the producers throw us a curveball and tell us each group has to have contestants from both day one and day two. This sends me scrambling. I couldn't find anyone who wanted me—a deep-singing country singer—in their group.

Until I find Jacee and his group of four. They're hesitant, but Jacee immediately invites me in.

"We can do five."

Things are looking fine until later that night when the team has decided Jacee is just not working out. I miss this drama because I'm in the bathroom changing into sweats. We've been told it's gonna be a long night, and I need to get comfortable. They've told him he really doesn't fit in with the rest of us. There aren't any specific reasons. It's just one of those "sorry but this isn't going to work out" moments. I'm not even with the group at the moment the decision is made. When I arrive, the damage has been done, but I could have done something about it.

I don't do a thing.

My mom, who had brought me a change of clothes, asks me what's going on.

"I just saw Jacee's mom, and she's been crying," Mom says. I tell her the group decided to let him go while I was changing into my sweats.

"I can't do anything! I wasn't even around when it happened!"

"Good Lord, Scott! You know you should have stuck up for him."

As we're talking, we see a cameraman approaching. No doubt they sense a little made-for-TV drama. We quickly change the subject and walk away.

Man, I feel like dirt. I let one of the nicest guys I met in the competition just walk away. And *I* just keep rehearsing. But then I can see a couple of faces suddenly looking at me like those ghosts that come to haunt Ebenezer Scrooge at Christmastime.

I think of my music minister at my church, Beth Hunnicutt, who's been working with me since pre-school. Then I think of my guitar teacher,

Gary Epperson. I can picture both of them watching this scene unfolding, wondering what in the world happened to Scotty.

EARLY INFLUENCES

Beth Hunnicutt, our music minister at First Baptist Garner, may have been the first person to ever put a microphone in my hand. From the time I could walk, "Ms. Beth," as we kids called her, was always giving me a part in our church plays. I actually first started singing in the preschool choir at FBC.

First Baptist Garner, on the outskirts of Raleigh, has a membership of about 1,300 and averages around 700 on Sundays at our three services. Of course, the congregation was smaller when I was young, but FBC has always had a very large music program. It was just natural to be a part of it. Both my parents were in the adult choir, while Ash and I were in the kids'. Our kids' musicals could have as many as a hundred children participating. There were sound, lights, and costumes—also Bible verse memorization and a lesson in everything we performed.

Whenever we drove around town—to school or wherever—we were usually listening to a CD so we could memorize a new church musical or a solo. My mom and dad sang solos too. We would listen to some cool, upbeat tunes at FBC—

music from Brooklyn Tabernacle, Steven Curtis Chapman, and Nicole C. Mullen. Once, driving through Garner, my mom had her music cranked up a little too loud. We were both belting out a rocking, contemporary Christian tune and didn't hear or see the Amtrak train coming through downtown Garner. She slammed on the brakes just as the safety arms were about to slam on our van. I was in the front seat and remember giving her a wide-eyed look and yelling, "Mom!"

"I guess we were enjoying that song a little *too* much," she said with a smile.

I couldn't have been more than seven or eight years old, but I still remember it like it was yesterday.

But that was our family. If we were in the car together, we were jamming out to something.

Later at First Baptist Garner, when I was in fifth grade, I played the part of Joseph in the Christmas play, singing "O Holy Night" and "A Strange Way to Save the World." By middle school, I felt comfortable enough to play my guitar with the youth group. Eventually, I sang with the First Baptist high school praise group called "Audience of One."

I remember kids in the youth group joking around and saying that whatever song Ms. Beth gave me, I'd make it sound country. I guess this was ideal training for Motown Week on *Idol* years later.

The very day I got home from the first Milwaukee audition in July 2010, I went on a mission trip to New York City with Ms. Hunnicutt and our youth group. We were able to attend an inner-city church where I sang "Long Black Train." After I finished, a smart-aleck kid at the church told me to "stick to your day job." I wish I could have told that kid, "Hey, I just made it through an *American Idol* audition. Watch the show and let's see what happens!" But of course, I was sworn to secrecy and didn't say a word.

Another important person in my musical apprenticeship was Gary Epperson, my guitar teacher from the time I was nine. A friend from church, Clay Fussell, told me about Gary. Luckily, Gary lived just a couple miles from my house. He was a high school teacher who played with a local band. He had built a cool studio in his basement. Gary says he noticed I had natural rhythm the first day I played for him.

For a while, Gary pursued being a musician in Nashville. He played me some of his tapes, and he was good! The music industry was a lot different back then, and he shared lots of stories about that. Gary said he gave it a good shot but eventually realized he was too old to become a breakout country artist. Plus, his wife didn't like Nashville, so moving back home to Garner was a no-brainer.

Gary's stories about the business side of

Nashville—the dog-eat-dog world—along with his fond and bittersweet memories of trying to make it in that world, sometimes made me wonder if I really wanted to make a run at it. It definitely sounded intimidating. Yet right before I went to Hollywood Week, Gary gave me a bit of advice.

"Don't stop," he said.

He was specifically talking about the moment I might find myself forgetting the lyrics of a song. Gary told me people who simply quit singing are always the first to be sent packing. But these two words take on a bigger meaning to me. They're a mantra of sorts to motivate me to keep going, no matter what.

I may be young, but I'm still smart enough to know incredibly talented guys like Gary didn't make it in Nashville for one reason or another. Life's like that. I know sometimes it's not fair.

> The first time we saw Scotty, we knew how talented and gifted he was. Driving down from Quebec to Nashville was worth the trip to meet him at *Idol*'s VIP experience. He was my great inspiration to learn guitar. He is such a genuine person and still is to this day. We love you, Scotty . . . forever.
>
> ROSE-LAURENCE SAMSON,
> McCREERIAN FROM QUEBEC, CANADA

You can only control the parts that have to do with you. When it comes to other people, however, you can be fair.

That's why I know I was wrong to let our group dump Jacee. I'm sure the two people who have spent more time than anyone else teaching and mentoring me in music would agree 100 percent with these thoughts.

I'm just not sure how to make things right again.

THE VIEW FROM HERE

On November 18, one of the show's executive producers, Nigel Lythgoe, went on the television show *The View* to talk about the upcoming season of *American Idol*. Up to this point, we hadn't told anyone I had made it through to the show's Hollywood Week. We hadn't even told my grandparents.

Mom had heard Nigel would be on *The View* and decided to tune in, hoping to hear some details about the new season. (Once again— homework.) Imagine her surprise when Nigel said he'd brought a clip of the new judges working together for the first time with "a young boy who's auditioning." There I was, singing the Travis Tritt tune "Put Some Drive in Your Country." That's the song that prompted the classic Steven Tyler line and the uproarious response from everyone on the set.

Mom couldn't believe it. She was absolutely speechless. She texted me at school. When I looked at my phone between classes, I saw not only the text from Mom, but other texts as well. People had heard I was on *The View* and were suddenly calling and asking questions.

Here we go, we all thought. *The cat is out of the bag.*

Now my friends and family knew what I was up to. So the pressure was on and the word was out, even if I wasn't supposed to talk about it.

YOU'VE GOT A FRIEND

During Hollywood Week, groups of kids would see me and walk over and say, "You're that kid they showed on *The View*, right?" From that point on, it felt like I had both a spotlight on me and a spot on my back.

I do end up making a friend right after arriving in Hollywood. I've been there for maybe five hours. Or maybe just five minutes. I'm not sure. But I find myself standing next to a smiling blonde-haired girl as we're waiting to go to confessional—the *Idol* confessional, not the sort you find at a church.

"What's your name?" she asks with a speed and enthusiasm that catch me off guard.

"Scotty. What's yours?"

"I'm Lauren. Where're ya from?"

Her questions go on.

"Where did you audition?"

"What song did you sing?"

"How old are you?"

Wow, this girl is like the Energizer Bunny!

It's only fitting I meet Lauren Alaina at the very beginning. Could this be some kind of fore-shadowing?

I remember her laughter while we were talking. It's the sort that makes you smile, the kind they call infectious. It makes competing against every-body, including her, just a little easier.

I wonder how long both of us will be around in this competition. But this is before I hear the girl sing. Once I hear that . . . dang. I'll know she'll be around for a long, *long* time with that voice. My mom is so impressed that she calls my aunt Barbara back home and tells her about Lauren.

"I don't know how far Scotty will go, but I think the winner will be this girl from Georgia."

SAY SOMETHING

I've always believed in speaking up when the time is right. Nobody will ever accuse me of being the most talkative person around. This certainly wasn't the case on *Idol* as Lauren and I got to know each other. She talked and I listened, and we both laughed a lot.

I might be quiet, but I will say something, however, if it's necessary.

I remember once in grade school, I got in trouble after the bus driver thought I was using curse words. I wrote her a letter to tell her the truth. It wasn't about ratting anybody out; it was simply setting the record straight.

Dear Ms. Brenda,
I am sorry for what other people might think, but I was not cursing. If you want to know the truth, then here it is.
A.J. has a calculator type thing that has letters on it. They were typing up cuss words on it. I was not. So if you could, I would like to be moved away from A.J. and the people that sit in front of me. I am sorry if I have bothered you.
P.S. Have a MEERY CHRISTMAS
Sincerely,
Scotty McCreery

On the night of the group performances, I find myself in the same predicament I was in on that school bus. I know I have to set the record straight for the judges and the rest of the kids competing. Even if it's to my own demise.

I don't see Jacee's performance with the group that finally accepted him. I also don't see him break down in tears after he learns he got through. All I know backstage as we're getting ready to walk out is something happened that created applause.

I'm suddenly nervous to step in front of the three judges who have always praised me (so far). There's a different vibe. I don't even have to wonder why.

"Did you guys have a member at one time who's missing?" Randy asks us.

"Not really missing," Clint Jun Gamboa says, the somewhat-designated leader of our group.

"Everything's cool," I say.

Clint keeps explaining the situation. "It just seems like his vibe was better with another group."

At the same time, Randy asks, "Who are we speaking about?"

"Can I just say something about Jacee?" I ask.

The crowd of contestants sitting in the audience learns from the judges we voted Jacee off our team and gives all of us one loud, collective round of boos. We deserve it. Steven Tyler knows we deserve it.

"You know, for that alone we should make y'all step back one."

We're not getting *any* love on this stage today. And I know we brought this on ourselves.

Say something, Scotty.

There are moments in your life when you have to forget about everything else and simply do the right thing. That doesn't mean the right thing won't hurt.

I have to speak my mind.

"I just want to go on record and say for me personally, I apologize for not sticking up for him. 'Cause I love all of y'all, but Jacee's the best kid in this whole competition."

Win or lose, it doesn't matter. My heart is pounding, but I have to say something. I'm better than the guy who let a great guy like Jacee be forced to walk away. I should have been stronger then, and I'm making amends now.

All I can do is set the record straight, apologize, accept the consequences, and move on.

WHAT IT MEANS

I've never tried to be known as the good kid or some kind of holy roller. Believe me, I am not Saint Scott. I've had the speeding ticket. During my glory days at NC State, my guys and I planned a birthday/back-to-school party for our room-mate, Andrew "Bird" Robinson—a party aptly named Birdapalooza. It was eventually shut down for noise and a wee bit of a traffic jam it caused in the area. When the police arrived, they told us, "Look, boys, we have to give you a ticket, but this is impressive."

My point in sharing the above is to tell you I'm a normal guy. If you're looking for Mr. Perfect, well, it's not me.

I do, however, know what my values are. These have come from my family and the church I've grown up attending. Those two things led me to finding the one Person I turn to for strength, guidance, and forgiveness.

I learned about Him at First Baptist in Garner.

All kids who grow up in a Christian church, of course, learn about Jesus. How He was born in a manger and why we celebrate Christmas. How Jesus healed the sick and gave to the poor. How Jesus died and rose again from the dead and that's why we celebrate Easter. I was taught these things and sang about them, but these things became personal at a youth retreat when I was around twelve.

Some may feel the Bible is full of fairy tales or is only for superstitious people. Not me. In my church group, we said the letters of B-I-B-L-E stood for "Basic Instruction Before Leaving Earth." I thought that was kinda cool. To me, the Bible is a guidebook, not a rule book.

I also learned the Bible is a history book, as well as a book of prophecies fulfilled through Jesus. For example, the Old Testament book of Micah says a ruler will be born in Bethlehem. Isaiah says the Messiah will be from "the house of David." Well, both Mary and Joseph, Jesus' earthly parents, were descendants of King David. Isaiah 53 says the Messiah will be "despised and rejected by mankind . . . pierced for our transgressions," and "by his wounds we are healed." To me that's full-on talking about Jesus. Doesn't get more real than that.

So at age twelve, while at this retreat, I knew I believed in Jesus, but I finally understood what it meant to be a sinner. Yeah, even good ole Scotty is a sinner. I realized Jesus Christ was born and lived on this earth to die for me. In the Old Testament, you read about people making animal sacrifices and giving offerings to God to atone for their sins. In the New Testament, we learn God sent Jesus, who would sacrifice *Himself* for *our* sins. Suddenly, Christmas and Easter—especially Easter—took on a whole new meaning. I thought about Christ on the cross taking on my sins, and that's when I turned my life over to Him.

I know there are all sorts of doubters who wonder where God is in our world. I've wondered the same thing at times. But God is in the same place He was when His Son died on the cross. Watching, waiting, hurting. I know people ask why God lets bad things happen. Why is God hard on us sometimes? I gotta believe it's because God loves us too much to leave us the way we are. There are lessons in our struggles. Some lessons we figure out; some we might not figure out until we're on the other side of heaven.

When I got back from the retreat, I told my pastor what happened and how I wanted others to know about my decision to follow Jesus. The next Sunday, I walked forward and made my commitment public. That's how we do it in a Southern Baptist church, anyway.

I didn't realize walking down that church aisle was the first of many times I'd show my faith in front of others. I didn't know all the things my decision meant at the time. All I knew was I was trusting God with my life and I was committed to following Him.

I think of the words of Jeremiah 29:11: " 'For I know the plans I have for you,' declares the LORD, 'plans to prosper you and not to harm you, plans to give you hope and a future.' "

Hope. A future.

These words encouraged me from a very young

age. And even years later, during Hollywood Week, I'm thinking of them again. I remind myself that God has plans, and they're good ones.

I have to believe it.

I also have to remain strong and remember the values I've grown up learning about my whole life. Like the warning from my favorite Josh Turner song: *Watch out, brother, for that long black train.*

I HOPE YOU NEVER, EVER DANCE AGAIN

I gotta believe God has a sense of humor when He arranges the way things in our lives happen.

One of these moments comes after the Jacee situation during Hollywood Week. It's round 3, and we're given a list of songs we can perform. I honestly don't know any of them. Not well. I choose a popular country song from the list, and I have only hours to learn it.

I can be a fast learner, but I sure don't learn this song fast. I'd grown up hearing the tune, but there's a difference between knowing a song and singing it.

When I end up performing "I Hope You Dance" by Lee Ann Womack, with the band accompanying me, well . . .

Would you believe me if I said I really felt inspired to write a few of my own lyrics?

The performance is a train wreck.

Sometimes you just strike out. But I remember what my guitar teacher Gary preached: "Don't quit; keep singing." And that's what I did.

They should've really voted me off right then and there. I leave the stage, find a seat, and suddenly feel severe disappointment. I've let down myself, my family, and everybody I know.

Man, I can do better than that.

I can already imagine people out there on social media typing those familiar two words: EPIC FAIL.

"Is this the end of the line?" I can imagine Ryan Seacrest saying. "There's no more babies locking their doors for Mr. McCreery. It's time to shut them for good on his young country soul."

Eventually, all of us contestants are divided into four groups. Each group is placed in a room. I wait and know it's all in God's hands—well, in Jennifer Lopez's, Steven Tyler's, and Randy Jackson's hands too. Once in the room, we all stare at each other, trying to figure out if we are in a "good room" or a "bad room." I see Jacob Lusk, who has brought it every single performance. That's a very good sign. And I spot Haley Reinhart. No way is she getting cut.

The judges walk in, and I swear there's not a sound in that room.

"You're all going through!"

Screams erupt as the room explodes with congratulations and hugs.

I'm safe . . . and surprised again. I walk up to Jennifer Lopez and thank her. I look her in the eyes and tell her, "Y'all should have cut me." She reassures me otherwise and gives me a hug. Weeks down the road, on live TV, she'll remind me of this moment.

VEGAS, BABY!

We board buses and head to the Mirage on the Vegas strip, where we'll be performing on the same stage where "The Beatles *Love* by Cirque du Soleil" is playing. I'm in a group with Lauren Alaina and Denise Jackson.

The Jacee incident is one of the lows. My rendition of "I Hope You Dance" is certainly another. But singing a classic Beatles tune ends up completing this terrible trifecta.

The first song we're given ends up being disastrous. The mentor we meet for the first time tells us to get a new song. He's Jimmy Iovine, the chairman of the major record label Interscope Geffen A&M.

He's the guy we all want to impress. So you take his advice. If he says jump, you don't even bother to ask "how high?" simply because you should already be up in the air.

That's another reason it's disappointing our

rendition of "Hello, Goodbye" doesn't go better. How could anything go wrong with a performance in Vegas on a Cirque du Soleil stage where we're coming out of a phone booth and singing a song made famous by the most iconic band *ever?* I have lots of experience with that, right?

The judges seem to have a collective sense of the mehs. They say the song didn't fit us. We get a "good try," which sounds a lot like a yawn. I had my best smile and my highest pitch. I thought trying something different would be good.

So the Vegas round ends, and we're called back on the stage to hear who survived.

Well, it's been fun. If I'm sent home, it's still been an incredible ride.

The votes are in, and Denise doesn't make it through. Lauren and I do.

I'm still hanging in there, but it feels like just barely.

A QUARTER PUERTO RICAN

One of the high moments of Hollywood Week—well, actually of the whole competition—comes after the Vegas round. We're in an old aircraft hangar for a solo round. I've just performed "Long Black Train." Jennifer Lopez shares with me her lovely smile and applause and then another compliment.

> Scotty, Lauren, and I were in Las Vegas for the Beatles round of *American Idol* during the middle of December. We stumbled on a man singing Christmas carols on the side-walk and decided to just join in on "Feliz Navidad." It was so genuine and fun, and I just remember being so happy to be with such great people.
>
> JACEE BADEAUX,
> *AMERICAN IDOL* SEASON 10

"You make a Bronx girl love country music," she says.

My heart's beating fast, and I stumble to find the words I want to say.

"My grandmother told you to—told *me* to tell you, Jennifer. I know you can't tell, but I'm a quarter Puerto Rican."

She laughs and loves it. "*That's* where that soul comes from."

"Yes, ma'am."

I could never have imagined, weeks later, my grandmother Paquita from San Juan, Puerto Rico, would get to meet the beautiful Ms. Lopez. It was Top 5 Week on *Idol*, and grandma Paquita is in the audience. The number one rule for audience members is "DO NOT APPROACH

THE JUDGES." However, Paquita McCreery marches to the beat of her own drum. She zips right over to Jennifer during a commercial break to have a conversation in Spanish. Before security can stop Paquita, Jennifer sees her and stops security from intervening. Jennifer looks at her and says, "I've been waiting to meet you!" What a moment for my grandmother!

But I digress. As the hangar round ends, we hope to learn our fate. It's the end of the year, but we're told we'll have to wait. We're left with an unwrapped box to be put under our Christmas trees but not opened until January.

THE GREEN MILE

After those highs and lows of Hollywood Week, the forty-one contestants who made it through had one final day of reckoning. This would come in the new year.

The final decision, which rests solely in the judges' hands, comes at the moment referred to as "the Green Mile." Some folks don't know this, but that long platform they make you walk that leads to the judges? It's actually a mile long.

Just kidding. But it sure feels like it as you step over the circles illuminated in green and make your way toward the judges for their final decision. Yes, or no.

Randy asks me while I'm sitting across from

them whether I had imagined this when I first auditioned. It's a hard question, because a part of me *did* see myself at this point. A part of me can picture winning the whole thing. People didn't realize by the time I appeared on *Idol*, I had been singing onstage since three, had gotten used to being on the pitcher's mound since around age ten, and during the last two and a half years had spent every school day in a classical chorus program, learning scales, vocal technique, and sight reading. I may not have looked the part, but I had a fair amount of experience performing in public. The big question was, "Will America like me?"

Then again, another part of me is continuing to ask that question I asked my pops in Milwaukee.

What am I doing here?

The main thing I want to convey is how honored I am to be in front of them right now. That's exactly how I feel.

"Hollywood was a little interesting," Randy says with a chuckle. "There were some highs and some lows."

Here's my chance to share more with them on my failure during that week.

"You know, for me personally, that whole night with Jacee—that was more about me not being the man I should have been. And not steppin' up when I should've stepped up for him. 'Cause he's a phenomenal kid. He didn't deserve that. That night, I just went back to my bed and cried. I wasn't the man I should've been. I didn't step up."

After telling me they've all been my fans from the very beginning, Randy says something I still think about to this day.

"That authenticity about the guy you want to be and the man you want to be. And you steppin' up. We love. We're big fans. Guess what that means?"

Yep.

It means a whole lot of things.

It means I'll be sharing this moment five years later in the pages of a book. It means there will be a whole lot of songs sung and written and performed. It means there will be so many doors opening and so many chances given.

So you're telling me there's a chance.

And it means God is good.

I know Randy, Steven, and Jennifer all think I can sing. But the whole steppin' up thing? What a surprise. I never dreamed anything positive would come out of something I felt so bad about.

Moments after hugging my parents and Ashley, celebrating making it to the Top 24, I find Jacee and give him a big hug. He looks like the brother I never had, proud to see I got through.

He's one of the many great people I meet on a journey that's about to begin.

Chapter Four

America's Storyteller

When Season 10 of *American Idol* begins airing on January 19, 2011, the worst-kept secret in my hometown of Garner is that I'll be on the show. Remember, *The View* episode aired two months earlier, and the buzz was growing. It was a faint one, but it was there. During this time, I was working at Lowes Foods. When I first applied in 2010, the manager saw I had won a couple of talent shows and asked if I'd ever tried out for *American Idol*.

"Actually I have."

"When was that?" she asked me.

"Well, it's happening now. But I can't say too much about it."

Months pass, and the day finally arrives when my first episode will air. I'm checking groceries, and I put a note on my register: "Watch an Employee from this Lowes Foods Tonight on *Idol*!"

When customers ask me if I'm talking about myself, I simply smile and say, "You have to watch for yourself."

By the time the Top 24 is announced, my family and friends throw a big party to celebrate making it to the live shows. All of the other shows had been taped and shown at a later date, yet all shows will now be airing in real time.

I've made it to the Top 24. I'm told I won't have a lot of time off—maybe Easter. I fly to Los Angeles, where I'll be busy for quite some time. Suddenly, I find myself transitioning from Scotty, the high school junior, to Scotty, the busy singer who'll be performing in front of millions. This new Scotty will still have to attend school at the studio, do homework, and have adult supervision, since I'm only seventeen.

Soooo very glamorous.

During the first half of 2011, I live in five different places. For a short while, the finalists are living in a mansion. Again, such a glamorous life. Except for the fact that we are hardly there because we have to be at either Interscope or CBS Studios.

The mansion is a beautiful place, but it's a bit cozy. The guys are together in one room and the girls in another. Lots of twin beds in these rooms resembling army barracks more than the accommodations of a music reality show. Some neighbors complain because Jacob Lusk sings outside in the rose garden. There's one laundry room to share. Mom actually jumps in and does some of the kids' laundry while they're at rehearsals.

The cameramen try to film us randomly in the mansion. As much as we liked the camera guys, sometimes we wanted our space. We'd see the approaching cameras and start talking about competing advertisers we knew they couldn't air. "Can someone get me a Pepsi?" "Love this new Verizon phone." Or "Need a Chevy?"

Still, it was pretty sweet living in the mansion. That's where I made that killer basketball goal from the second-floor balcony. For the record, that shot took me three tries.

Then came the rumor the mansion is haunted. What actually happened (and Stefano Langone and Jacob Lusk tell it best) is a storm hit one night while we slept. With lightning flashing and wind howling, the doors and windows of the guys' bedroom blew open. Freaked us out! Imagine waking up and seeing bedspreads and sheets flapping as the wind and rain whip through the room. For a second, it *is* pretty scary. The reaction of my housemates is hysterical, and I get a good chuckle out of it as well. Some media outlets, however, hear about it and print a story saying the mansion is haunted.

In the midst of all this, I'm staying focused, always thinking ahead to my next performance. I spend a lot of time thinking about the songs I'm going to sing. Take the very first one I end up performing during the semifinal round of the Top 24. This will be the first time I sing live in front of the country, and I know I need to pick a great tune. There's no theme, and we can choose any song.

I pick "Letters from Home" by John Michael Montgomery.

Ah, another country tune by the country boy.

That's what some casual viewers might think. But it's a great song, and it fits what America is dealing with. It's patriotic and tells a story about letters from a mother, girlfriend, and father to a soldier serving far from home.

"Son, you make me proud," a key line goes.

I know a lot of viewers are living exactly what this song is about. If I can get people who watch the show to love the song as much as I love it, I'll be able to connect with them. That's why I choose songs that not only I can relate to, but that the country can relate to as well.

This is a competition; it's not a vacation. And no offense to the fine folks at Lowes Foods, but I'd much rather be working hard singing in LA than working hard behind a cash register in Garner.

A STORY IN THE SONGS

The new format for *American Idol* on Season 10 starts on March 1, 2011, with the semifinal round in which I sing "Letters from Home." Twelve males and twelve females participate in this round, each picking songs of their own choosing. The viewers get to phone in and choose who they want to continue in the competition. The top five males and top five females advance to the finals.

Before the finals begin, there's one more round thrown in there. The judges pick six of the contestants who weren't voted through to the finals. These singers will compete in the wild card round. After each singer performs, the judges will pick three of them to advance, making the final group consist of thirteen singers.

Each week features a different theme related to the songs we have to choose from. There will be everything from songs from the year we were born to ones sung by Elton John. This makes it both exciting and challenging. As always, the choice of song can be one of those make-or-break things in the competition.

Here are some things you might not know about some of my song choices.

Starting with the Top 13, we get to pick a song by one of our personal idols. My choice is easy.

"The River" is a Garth Brooks classic. After watching Garth's DVDs, I finally had the chance to see him in 2012 at the Wynn in Las Vegas. We bought tickets and contacted my manager to see if she could arrange for me to meet this musical hero of mine after his show. Near the end of Garth's performance, a young lady slipped down my row and tapped me on the shoulder.

"I'm August Brooks," she said. "Would you like to meet my dad?"

My family and I were in Las Vegas for the ACM Awards show. We happily left our seats and were taken backstage, where we got to meet August's dad, the legendary Garth Brooks, along with the lovely Trisha Yearwood. It was an incredible night.

During each week of competition on *Idol*, it's clear Jimmy Iovine believes in me, and he continues to help me grow with each song I perform. We're working with Don Was, a famous producer and musician I immediately connect with. Don tells me he worked with Garth Brooks also. The fact that I can be in a studio working with guys like Jimmy and Don is incredible.

Another song I choose is a Travis Tritt ballad, trying my best to be a young romantic. Okay, maybe not, but I'm hoping that America is hearing and seeing a lot of passion in the performance of "Can I Trust You with My Heart?"

Motown Week is the next theme for the Top 11. I have a hard time finding a country tune in that genre. I don't seem to have a hard time countryfying one of the songs. I pick a classic Stevie Wonder tune, "For Once in My Life." Jimmy Iovine tells me to not sing it so smoothly that I come off sounding like a lounge singer. He counsels me to keep Stevie Wonder's intensity while retaining my smooth country soul sounds.

I attack the song. The audience loves it, the judges love it, and America seems to love it too when I get through to the next round.

I'm not changing. I'm sticking with what I love. "Staying in my lane." Keeping it country.

Even when Elton John Week comes along. I get to do "Country Comfort." Not only do I sing an early Elton song, but it's from the album *Tumbleweed Connection*, which was influenced by both country music and the American West. Don Was and Jimmy Iovine suggest I do the second verse about the factory closing down instead of the verse about the grandmother—until I tell them my reason for picking that one.

"My grandma's actually going to be in the audience this week," I say.

They can only laugh and agree with me.

"That works," Jimmy says with a confident nod.

When I reach the part of the song that mentions her, I give Grandma Janet a shout-out that I love her. She's on national television and gets to show off her beautiful and proud smile.

How could I *not* do such a perfect song?

Rock and Roll Hall of Fame Week comes when only nine of us remain. I simply smile and think, *Here we go.* I get to do a song by the King of Rock and Roll himself.

That's all right.

I tell America in one of the interviews shown before I sing that I'll be doing something different, that it's not going to be the country Scotty everybody knows. But come on, now.

What's that saying again?

You can take the boy outta the country, but you

95

can't take the country outta the boy. Especially when it's Elvis, that great country boy himself.

Right before I perform, I receive one of the coolest compliments ever. Priscilla Presley happens to be in the audience. She comes over before the cameras go live.

"Scotty," she says in a whisper, "can I tell you something?"

"Sure."

"Elvis would have loved you."

Well, roll me over and shoot me dead . . .

Talk about a motivational speech before my song. And the speech only lasted a couple seconds.

Priscilla and photographer Christopher Ameruoso would later ask me to be photographed in a book they coauthored titled *Shades of Elvis*. In this project, celebrities were photographed wearing Elvis's actual sunglasses. I can't even describe how incredible it was to wear those sunglasses.

I have a lot of fun with the Elvis classic. If you watch the YouTube video, you can see the judges echoing excitement and giving positive feedback about trying something different. Randy says anyone who thought I was a one-trick pony who could only do country was wrong. He went on to say he'd never seen this side of me. Steven reacts the same, saying how great it was I brought Elvis in the house and how he hoped I could bring that old nostalgic type of music back. *I do too, Steven, I do too.*

But Jennifer Lopez's comments really crack me up. She asks if I watch rap or hip-hop, because she's feeling a little flavor! I should have said, "It's my Puerto Rican Latino blood coming out!" Performing "That's All Right" confirms I'm continuing to grow more comfortable moving around the stage and moving behind the judges, all the while singing and smiling, telling my story to America.

I continue to select songs that have an underlying message.

"Letters from Home" is my greeting to the great beating heart of America.

"The River" is sharing my hopes and dreams with the audience.

"Can I Trust You with My Heart?" is me asking

It was March 2011 when I first saw Scotty in *American Idol*. I wasn't really a big fan of the show, but on the day Scotty appeared as one of the Top 24, a friend called me and insisted I tune in and watch "this kid with an amazing voice. His name is Scotty." He sang "Letters from Home." This song I'd never heard before and that amazing voice started it all.

ANGELITA FLORES,
McCREERIAN FROM TAIWAN

the viewers that very question. Can I continue to reveal parts of myself to you?

"For Once in My Life" shares what's in my soul—that I suddenly feel I have this love of the viewers by my side, and I'm going to fight to keep it. It's the love of singing and performing, and nobody can take it from me.

"Country Comfort" reminds everyone I have those sweet, old-fashioned country sounds in my bones.

And "That's All Right" reminds everybody who inspired me in this journey that everything is really and truly all right.

I'm telling a story, and each week it keeps getting better. That is, until Songs from the Movies Week comes along.

The story suddenly goes south.

BACK HOME

I never stop thinking of everybody back home in Garner, North Carolina. Each night after the show is taped, I go to my room and check online to see what's happening back home. There's a viewing party that started when the Top 24 were performing. At that time, maybe thirty or forty people came to our local performing arts center to watch *Idol*. A guy would post a video from each viewing party. Soon, there were several hundred attending. Eventually, the crowd got so big they had to move it to Garner High's gym.

Seeing the faces and smiles of all the people watching the show and cheering me on filled me with lots of things—joy, hope, courage, determination. More than anything, they simply *filled* me, especially after an exhilarating and exhausting day.

Seeing my family and friends cheer for me was great. Seeing the Blue Crew cheer for me, with the same cheers I used to yell for our football team—that was priceless. It always led me to think the same thing.

Man, I wish I could be two places at once.

In a weird way, I was actually a million places at once. Or at least on millions of TV screens. But my heart was always there, back home in Garner, back where they were cheering on one of their own.

EVERYBODY'S TALKIN'

Songs can take journeys of their own, just like all of us can. A weathered and well-traveled tune found its way to my doorstep by the time I made it to the Top 8. It had quite the history, and it seemed like the perfect song choice.

But perfect is in the eye of the beholder.

Sometimes great art is formed by accident or as an afterthought. Hundreds of songs written in fun or created in a matter of minutes or initially rejected by a label end up becoming classics. One of these songs is "Everybody's Talkin'."

In 1966, a musician named Fred Neil was recording a folk-blues album in Los Angeles and wanted to get back home to Miami. The problem was he hadn't written enough songs. So his manager told him to write one more song, and then he'd be allowed to leave. So Fred took five minutes to create the song, recorded it in one take, and then took off for home.

It's no coincidence that the song itself is about a man talking about going where the sun is shining and getting away from all these people.

Fred Neil's life seemed to follow in the footsteps of his song, since he hated anything to do with fame and eventually became a recluse in the late 1960s.

But songs—well, sometimes they have lives of their own.

Fast-forward a couple years to when a singer by the name of Harry Nilsson heard the song and put it on his third album. Not long after that, a director made a film and put Harry Nilsson's rendition of this song in the working print since he wanted a song like that one. The director kept the song in his film. And that's when a classic was born.

That's also how I come into the story.

NOT JUST ANOTHER SONG

"How about this Harry Nilsson song?" Jimmy Iovine asks me.

This week's theme is Songs from the Movies. Jimmy plays me a song from the list, and I nod. I like it. So I begin to learn the song. It fits my style and my voice.

Soon after, I record the song in the studio since it will be released on iTunes after the show airs. As usual, I have to tape a preshow interview in which I tell why I picked this song. As I start my interview, the cameramen ask me if I've seen the movie it came from.

"Nah. Why don't you guys just tell me about it, and I'll repeat it on camera," I say.

"It's from *Midnight Cowboy*. Came out in the late sixties. Won some Academy Awards, including Best Picture."

"That's cool," I say.

"It's the first X-rated film to ever win an Oscar. It's about a male prostitute in New York City who becomes friends with a homeless con man."

Wait . . . what?

At first I think they're joking. They have to be joking, right? But after I ask them if they're serious, it becomes apparent they are.

I'm singing the theme song from that *film?*

We're long past the whole deciding about a song, yet there's no question whether or not I'm going to sing it. I can't. I won't. I'm not trying to be high maintenance.

"It's no big deal," they tell me.

"It's been covered a bunch of times," one of the producers says. "By everybody. The Beach Boys and Jimmy Buffett and even Stevie Wonder."

But it doesn't matter, because I know what will happen once I sing it. The same thing that's happened every week. A lot of people will discover a song for the first time, even if it's an all-time classic. They'll Google who sang it and where it came from. My fans include eighty-five-year-old grandmothers and ten-year-old kids.

I don't want them going to check out an X-rated movie. And I sure don't want people to think I'm watching X-rated movies in my spare time. I'm not trying to be some kind of movie critic (or holier-than-thou); I'm just trying not to send any sort of wrong message to anyone.

Soon after this conversation, I decide to slip away and have some time by myself. Just to think about things and pray and figure out exactly what to do.

DECISIONS

I sit in the McDonald's on Santa Monica Boulevard with my regular order of two crispy Chicken Snack Wraps and fries. I stare out at the street and watch the cars pass by. All these different people steering their vehicles and living their lives. So many people just passing by.

I'm stuck in the same thought that's churning over and over.

I can't start compromising now. I can't. I won't.

The song I sang—the one I recorded—seems to haunt me. The words seem so crazy, so ironic.

"Everybody's talkin' at me. I don't hear a word they're saying. Only the echoes of my mind."

And somehow, in some crazy twist of fate, this is exactly what's happened. All the people back there say I *have* to sing the song, that there's no way I can back out now. But I'm not hearing them. All I can hear are the other thoughts telling me I can't perform it live in front of millions.

Why in the world would they pick *that* song for me?

Lord, is this a test? A trial of sorts?

I don't hear God's voice in this McDonald's. I do hear someone calling out for a supersize, but I don't think there's anything divine about that.

Maybe you can just sing it and nobody will comment on it or even care. An X-rated movie in 1969 might even be rated R these days.

It's a beautiful song, but there's more to singing it than the simple song. There's a story. There's a spotlight on something I don't feel comfortable turning the light toward. Sure, I get that there's all kinds of issues in the world, but I want to reflect things that reflect me.

I ask a hundred questions, but I answer all of them in the same way.

I want to sing a different song. If I gotta sing a song from a movie, it needs to be from a movie I can relate to.

Sure, I want an easy way out. I want to just go with the flow. But I know I can't.

I know I won't.

There are a dozen people—no, more than a dozen people I'm thinking about. People who would wonder what I'm thinking. People who might question what's happening.

Even my folks ask, "Are you making a mountain out of a molehill?"

I decide no. It's not one of those "let's see what they say" kind of noes; it's a no. I don't care what happens. I'm not singing the song on TV and I'm not talking about the movie and maybe everybody will be talkin' about me and that's fine because I'm not doing it.

I sip the water and miss the sweet tea I normally order back home.

I miss the South, and I miss Garner. But missing those things doesn't mean I have to forget about them.

JUST SAY NO

Jimmy Iovine is one of the reasons I loved the *American Idol* experience. Having a chance to

104

simply meet the man and spend time listening to his critique of my singing and song choices has been simply invaluable. I've had a chance to learn more about his career, and I deeply respect the guy.

To say Jimmy had humble beginnings in the record industry is putting it mildly. Raised in Brooklyn, he basically got his start sweeping floors at a New York recording studio and making tea and coffee. In a commencement speech Jimmy once gave at the University of Southern California, he said this about making tea and coffee: "It got me in the same building with John Lennon, who, after the fiftieth cup of tea I served him, felt my enthusiasm and willingness to learn and allowed me to sit in on his sessions."

Jimmy did exactly that, which led to his reputation for being able to find that perfect sound for the musicians he worked with. Jimmy ended up being the engineer on the defining Bruce Springsteen album. As Jimmy said in that speech, "*Born to Run* became a landmark album. If you don't know it, ask your parents."

For the rest of the seventies and eighties, he worked as an engineer and producer with many famous artists—Stevie Nicks, Tom Petty, U2, Bob Seger.

In 1989, Jimmy helped start Interscope Records. This successful record label had groundbreaking and envelope-pushing musicians such as Nine

Inch Nails and Dr. Dre. Interscope also led the way in the surge of producing hip-hop music by starting Death Row Records. Jimmy was instrumental in the start of a young rapper's career—Eminem. Jimmy would help produce the Oscar-winning movie *8 Mile*, starring the young musician.

After hearing stories and learning about Jimmy's incredible career, it's crazy to think I'm in the same studio with him, making music. John Lennon, Bruce Springsteen, Dr. Dre, and—oh, yeah—Scotty McCreery. Jimmy's been a big supporter of mine from the very start.

That's why my text to him is really going to be hard for me.

I text Jimmy and another person I greatly respect—Nigel Lythgoe, one of the primary producers on the show. I have to tell them what I've decided.

I'm not singing the song.

Their replies are quick and to the point.

Sorry, you have no choice.

The show is in two days.

I've always wondered what that line in the sand might look like, and I realize I've already drawn it.

With all due respect, I won't go on stage.

We go back and forth, but I guess they realize they can't get me to perform if I physically won't get out there and sing. I'm not sure if they've had a situation like this. Sure, I'm the nice kid from North Carolina who is polite and always positive. But I'm not sure anybody, including Jimmy and Nigel, knows how strong I can be. Maybe it's called strong-willed. Or stubborn. I don't have to call it anything except remaining true to who I am.

That night at ten o'clock, they send a car to get me and bring me to the recording studio, where Jimmy and Don Was await to record a new song in a hurry. I am beyond grateful they are willing to work with me. The producers aren't happy, however, because this is costing them more time and money.

I have to pick a different movie song quickly. I think of my favorite artists who have also acted in movies. I think of Elvis, but I had just done an Elvis song. Then I remember George

Strait in *Pure Country*. One of my favorite Strait songs is in that movie—"I Cross My Heart." I choose this song to sing.

There's a line in the song that says I'll promise to give all I've got to give. Once again, the lyrics aren't lost on me. Not a bit. I'm still telling a story about who I am and the journey I'm on. After I finish singing it, the judges—well, they seem to like it. Quite a bit.

"America, look at this guy right here," Randy says pointing at me. "A star is born on this stage."

He talks about how I've grown since my first audition. Randy's right, but not just with my singing. I'm having to grow up *fast* for a seventeen-year-old. Like having to say no to a television executive and music label executive, both of whom have been in the industry longer than I've been alive.

It doesn't matter, however. Age is one of those relative things. Sometimes people have to grow up fast. That doesn't mean you can't stand up for yourself.

I will learn I'll have to be a businessman. I'll have to take stands and even get into arguments. I'm all about listening to people's opinions—I *have* to. I know I don't know everything. But I do know myself, and I do know how to say the word *no*.

Even nice guys can say that word from time to time.

CONSTRUCTIVE CRITICISM

The judges of Season 10, sometimes accused of being too nice, eventually have to be a little hard on me. The time was coming. It couldn't be a lovefest the whole season. So my day of reckoning with my Puerto Rican crush comes during the Top 7 when I perform the one song I probably enjoy singing *the most* in the whole competition. It's true.

It's also the song that makes Gary, my guitar teacher, believe I'm headed home after—well, let's just say a not-so-stellar Scotty moment on the show.

I don't think it's that bad a performance. I love the song.

My Blue Crew at school loved to crank up this song. I remember being in Spanish class with my friend Kyle Wiggins, talking about this song. We'd make classic country CDs in our free time. "Swingin' " by John Anderson was one of my favorite songs. I remember telling Kyle, "If I ever get on *American Idol*, I'm singing this song."

So when it's the Top 7 and we have songs from the twenty-first century to perform, I discover a loophole. The original song came from the 1980s, but LeAnn Rimes sang a version of it in 2010.

I know things are going to go bad when I see Jennifer Lopez make a face during my rehearsal for "Swingin'." Deep down, I know this isn't going to be pretty. I share my thoughts with Mom before the show goes live.

"I'm about to get beat up," I tell her.

We spend a few minutes talking about how I'll handle any criticism. I haven't received much of it since Hollywood Week. Now I'm wondering if that's been a blessing or a curse.

"Just think of being back on the mound pitching at Middle Creek," Mom says about our rival school. "Just remember how much flack you'd get from their dugout."

It's a good point. I've realized all those years of pitching have given me thick skin. If I had a nickel for every time I've been heckled while pitching . . . But dang—at the most, a hundred folks might be watching me pitch. I'm about to be criticized in front of twenty million. Even so, baseball taught me how to get up in front of everybody and simply do my job. Whether it's hoping to strike out batters or hoping to strike a chord with the judges.

"Swingin' " doesn't exactly strike a chord, however. After my rendition on live television, Jennifer Lopez doesn't give me her trademark grin I've been accustomed to receiving.

You're getting spoiled, Scotty-boy.

She tells me at this point in the competition, she expects more. Especially from all the songs I could have chosen. She wants something more exciting, something that pushes me.

"You know I love you, Scotty," Jennifer says.

Randy echoes her statement, saying he feels like it was safe and boring from me. The boobirds in the audience come out, like they always do when the judges become a little more critical of any contestant.

What stings the most is that my boys from high school—the Blue Crew, all wearing their royal blue Garner baseball shirts with pride—are front and center in the audience tonight, having flown in from North Carolina. I can just imagine the sort of ribbing I'm going to hear from them after this show is over.

You sure swung and missed tonight, Scotty!

I don't take this as criticism but simply as a chance to learn something. Could I have chosen a better song? Sure.

Thankfully, America still votes me through after what might have been a safe and lackluster performance.

MENTORS

Off-camera moments are some of those I'll remember the most from my *Idol* experience. Like when Beyoncé stands with her mother off set and calls me over.

"Scotty," she says, "come here, boy."

When I walk over to the women, they're both sweet and charming.

"I just love you, boy," Beyoncé says, adding a "woooh" that surely makes me blush.

It's pretty nerve-racking and pretty cool meeting all these celebrities. But those star-struck nerves leave you pretty quickly when you sing in front of three of the biggest names out there your very first time. I've grown used to being in front of lots of famous folks, talking and singing only inches away from them. I've come to realize famous folks are real and normal people just like everyone else.

For example, when I met President Obama, the first thing I did was joke with him about his NCAA tourney picks. I told him he needed to show my Wolfpack more love. At a fund-raiser, Emmitt Smith of Super Bowl fame asked to have his picture taken with me, and I just about died. *Emmitt Smith knows me?* After the *Idol* show in New Jersey, I met the governor, Chris Christie, who had brought some teenagers to the show. He shared some insight on how my life might change as a celebrity and then gave me his cell phone number. *What a normal dude,* I thought.

Doesn't matter if it's a musician, professional athlete, or politician. People are people. Yet it's always nice when they surprise you with their generosity. And when they seem to honestly want to help you.

Babyface, for example, really preached to not rely on the deep side of my voice. He encouraged me to try songs that were out of my comfort zone.

Sometimes Steven Tyler showed up at rehearsals and gave me his thoughts. He definitely didn't have to come, but Steven was interested and engaged. Sometimes I'd be singing, and he'd tell the band to stop midway through the performance so he could share some ideas or work with the guys. Once during a rehearsal, he came over and said, "Scotty, really milk that bridge." Steven didn't *have* to care, but he did.

So many people I'd seen on television and listened to their music—people like will.i.am, Sheryl Crow, Marc Anthony, and even Lady Gaga—helped educate me about singing,

---

After reaching the Top 4 of *American Idol*, we were treated to a luxury Hollywood spa day. Being the two small-town, home-grown guys Scotty and I are, this wasn't our forte, so after our massages and facials, we stumbled upon the pool-sized indoor hot tub. Donning our single-use mesh swim-suits, we got tired of relaxing and started doing cannonballs and making noise. The management had to come out and yell at us to shut up and relax!

JAMES DURBIN,
AMERICAN IDOL, SEASON 10

performing, and opening my mind to other genres.

I've suddenly skipped my junior year of high school and am earning a master's degree in Music 101.

GOING HOME

Each week, we have to say good-bye to someone else. It's the reality, but the longer I'm in Los Angeles, the more difficult it is to see them leave. These fellow contestants became friends first. Now they're family. We're in this busy bubble with the rest of the country watching. We're having fun, working hard, and somehow trying to stay normal. It's hard to know what normal looks like anymore.

The Top 7 turns to Top 6, and the number keeps going down. All the while, I feel confident. Not cocky or arrogant or entitled. I just never step on the stage feeling worried about the outcome.

I've been singing for America for a couple months now. How can I even *begin* to complain about or dread what might happen next?

The Top 6 results, however, give the Scotty fans a bit of a heart attack. I have to say—it did make me a bit nervous. I'm standing next to Casey Abrams, and Ryan is about to announce one of our names.

"The person who leaves the competition tonight on *Idol* . . ."

I don't hear my name. But it doesn't make it easy to give my friend a hug and join the remaining contestants in their seats. Nobody wants to see him go. Nobody wants to see any of us go home. Not now. Not after lasting this long.

Someone like Casey—this talented guy with a big smile and an infectious sense of humor—makes this journey all the better.

I remember learning something after this night—something many viewers might not catch. Ryan Seacrest reveals after the Top 5 results that I'd never been in the Bottom 2. They were simply shuffling things up.

This gives me another little push. A big one, actually. I'm really honestly believing I can win this thing.

And since I'm *not* going home . . .

I gotta go big.

I think of Coach Pake and my last game I pitched.

Let me finish the game. Let me keep pitchin'.

That's my hope and my prayer.

Chapter Five

Prayers, Plans, and Promises

So there's this chance. I decide to go ahead and check the weather next week to see what it looks like if it happens.

I had made it into the Top 4, and Results Night this week is extra special.

For *American Idol* aficionados, they know *exactly* what that means.

The Top 3 get the hometown visits.

That's why I'm checking to see what the weather in Garner, North Carolina, looks like. Because the day after you hear the results from the show, you head back home. Each person gets to go back to their hometown to visit friends and family and perform in front of everybody. *Idol* sends a film crew to capture every single, glorious moment.

So, let's see . . .

Friday, May 13. The day before a possible hometown visit.

100 percent chance of rain and thunderstorms.

Sunday, May 15. The day after a possible hometown visit.

100 percent chance of rain and thunderstorms.

And Saturday? Well, come on. If they could say 150 percent chance, I'm sure the weather forecasters would issue that.

I looked at the report on my computer and shook my head.

That sucks.

If I get to go back home to Garner, it would *literally* be raining on my parade.

Yes, that would mean I'd be in the Top 3, and yes, I'd be bringing *Idol* to North Carolina. How can I complain? But I know the reality. If there's a downpour—and you can bet your bottom dollar on this happening—then we'll have to move my concert to a smaller venue. Folks coming out to see me perform might not be able to see the show.

This anxious, "I can't do a single thing about it" feeling inside of me doesn't go away. I'm dejected and angry, and I know I gotta let it go. I gotta do what the cliché says:

Let go and let God.

I'm not trying to live out a bumper sticker here. What I'm trying to do is live out my faith. So in my hotel room, I grab my NIV Bible and decide to open it. Since I've been here on the show, it's not like I've been immersed in some kind of Bible study. I sure haven't been spending Wednesday nights and Sunday mornings in church, like my routine is back in Garner. Even so, it's not unusual to reach for the Word when I need some inspiration or direction.

On this night, I simply open my Bible to a random page and play biblical roulette.

The very first verse I read—the first verse my eyes are drawn to—is Amos 4:7.

"I also withheld rain."

Wow, did I really read that?

Now I know what you're thinking. *Sure, Scotty.* But this really happens. I open up my Bible, and this verse pops out of it.

Since Mom is in the apartment with me, I tell her what just happened. She doesn't tell me I'm crazy. All Mom does is nod and tell me the most important thing I can do.

"Pray about it," she says.

So that night, I pray to God. I'm not some quasi-celebrity on the verge of something big talking to some nice higher power asking for a big, fat favor.

I'm standing before the throne of the Almighty Maker of the heavens and the earth and every single thing ever created, including my family and myself and my deep voice. I ask God for His will to be done. I pray that if—and that's *if*—I make it back to Garner for a hometown visit, I ask God to do exactly what this verse says.

"Could you please keep the rain from falling?" I ask my heavenly Father. "Let it rain somewhere else."

Maybe this is a selfish prayer. But my coming back to Garner won't be about Scotty McCreery. I know that for a fact. It will be all about Garner itself.

I don't want the weather to tarnish Garner's victory lap. I want their celebration to be as big, bold, and blessed as possible.

The great thing about praying to God is that He can see into your heart and know exactly what you're asking for and why you're asking. There are no hidden motives or agendas. Not with God. He's not only watching behind the camera; He's also the producer listening with headphones and the stagehand waiting behind the curtain. God knows everything about each request we offer up.

This request isn't for me or my family. It's for Garner. It's for the people who have been here with me from day one.

LAKE BENSON PARK, MAY 14, 2011

God answers prayer. My *Idol* experience allows me to see this, week after week. It's an incredible thing.

And so it happens. I made the Top 3. I've also come back home.

A funny thing has happened to Garner since I left. It seems like everybody has lost their minds.

Why? Well, because I see my smiling mug on a sign that's bigger than the town sign of Garner it sits next to. Everywhere I go, I see my name.

It's on a billboard and on signs in people's yards and lining the street like the names of politicians. My neighbors across the street actually have a "Scotty for President" sign in their front yard. I see all sorts of signs in the backs of trucks and cars, welcoming me back home.

I know nobody's crazy around here. They're just excited about one of their own making it on *Idol* and showing off their town. Now I'm back, and I get to share some of the love I've been getting.

I cannot wait.

PREPARATIONS

I'll probably never know all the work that went into my hometown visit. Even the few details I know boggle my mind at how everyone simply stopped what they were doing and created a big party for my homecoming. I hadn't even won the competition, but Garner sure acted like I had. It was pretty awesome.

A few weeks before I made the Top 3, Neal Padgett of the Garner Chamber of Commerce reached out to my parents just to ask that big question: "What if?" Of course, we've been asking it every day for the last year, it seems. *What if I make it past Milwaukee? What if I get through Hollywood Week? What if I survive "Swingin'"?* So it's reasonable for Garner to ask. It takes some time to plan a party, especially a big one.

My mom is always so resourceful. She's also a Garner chamber member and recommends to Neal that the town simply implement their existing annual July 3 symphony and fireworks festivities plan. For as long as I can remember, Garner has hosted the North Carolina Symphony at Lake Benson Park every July 3. Thousands attend to hear a great show and see incredible fireworks. The town already knew how to plan for parking and shuttles at Lake Benson Park, and there was plenty of manpower to assist with handling large crowds.

With this strategy in mind, Garner still had to take off like some kind of Olympic sprinter once I made it to the Top 3. A committee had been formed weeks earlier, made up of people from our chamber of commerce, town government, local churches, my high school, local businesses, and even local law enforcement agencies. I'd learn later the chamber had been very proactive and even had a conference call with the Little Rock, Arkansas, Chamber of Commerce, which had planned a homecoming visit for Season 8 winner Kris Allen. But it didn't matter how much work the Garner group could do in advance. Garner still didn't know if I was actually going to make it. Everybody believed—and some say they knew without a doubt—I'd be in that Top 3.

Still, they couldn't pull the trigger on any kind of formal announcement until I got through to the next round. *Two days* before the event.

The wonderful folks at our church go into action right away. First Baptist of Garner finds a hundred volunteers who will wear yellow "Team Scotty" T-shirts to assist the crowds. Garner High actually wanted to host the event, but with needs like parking, restrooms, and sound requirements, Lake Benson Park made a lot more sense.

Another one of those crazy "what if?" things we learned before I made the Top 3—*Idol* told us we'd have to stay at a hotel near the airport. This meant I couldn't even sleep in my own bed during my hometown visit. How crazy was that? Our family was bummed, but we also realized it made sense for safety and security reasons.

Even then, it was hard to understand just how big this whole thing had gotten. I'd been busy inside the *Idol* bubble, so it was hard to fathom the momentum back in North Carolina.

Garner wasn't the only group celebrating my homecoming. A few weeks earlier, during Rock and Roll Hall of Fame Week, I'd been wearing a T-shirt that read, "It's Bo Time!" while being filmed. It wasn't unusual for me to be wearing this shirt, since Bojangles' was my favorite restaurant in the whole world. When the team at Bojangles', based in Charlotte, saw the clip that night, they went absolutely crazy. I didn't even realize my "Bo" shirt had been shown on television. It was the start of a very beautiful relationship with the chain.

The day we were in Garner for our homecoming visit, Bojangles' brought a fully catered meal for all of the *Idol* personnel, our police escorts, and our family to enjoy right before the Lake Benson performance. And Bojangles' had even sent boxes of their special biscuits to CBS Studios for us contestants on the show.

Southerners sure do know how to show their love. That includes enough chicken and biscuits to last for days.

SCOTTYMANIA

So surreal. Two words that could sum up an autobiography I might write forty years from now. I know life isn't always going to be like this—this might be the one and only time it's *ever* like this. But suddenly I know how Elvis or the Beatles might have felt.

The busy agenda for the day begins at 94.7 WQDR, my favorite radio station I'd grown up listening to. During the *Idol* run, they renamed themselves Scotty 94.7. WQDR had done an awesome job promoting me while I was on the show. I wasn't able to call in to the station much because of my schedule. During the show, I was on West Coast time, so when their morning show started at 6:00 a.m., it was just 3:00 a.m. in LA. The station, however, kept the *Idol* promotion amped by regularly featuring family, friends, mentors, and even the Garner mayor on their morning show. This kept the whole triangle area of North Carolina hyped about the show.

So I'm finally back on my home turf, getting ready to see the incredible team at Curtis Media and WQDR. They welcome me into the small studio that's packed with as many fans as possible.

"Scotty is in the house!" Mike Wheless, one of the morning hosts, shouts when we're live on the air. "How does it feel to be back home?"

"This is just amazing, man. I would have never expected this kind of turnout this early in the morning."

They tell me fans had arrived the night before in vans just to be able to watch me during the interview. Arriving *in the rain*. Yes, there's a little rain outside. It's crazy. We talk about the previous Thursday night when James Durbin and I were the last two left standing.

"Everybody wants to know," says Marty "The One Man Party" Young, another announcer. "We were all on the edge of our seats going NOOOO—what was it like? You and James left on the stage. What was going through your mind?"

"For me there, I was just trying to get the lyrics right for my exit song," I tell him.

Someone gives me an "awww" in the background.

"It's a pretty bad feeling," I say. "But James—he's a trooper. He's a true performer. And I'm just blessed to still be in it."

I get to answer questions about some of the people I've met—like Lady Gaga and Steven Tyler. They ask me the biggest thing I've missed about Garner.

"I've just missed the people," I say.

More questions come from fans, like which of the idols do I wish had made it to the Top 3.

"Man, I miss them all. We all got tight. Like one big family."

I do an Elvis impersonation (of course) and then share the favorite songs I performed on *Idol* ("That's All Right" and "Gone"). They ask who I'd like to sing with me in the finale.

"Maybe if Elvis is alive and living in Las Vegas, like they say he is—maybe he can come out and sing with me," I say.

I'm teasing.

Well . . .

Unless Elvis is listening.

I get to share with everybody about an email I got from my idol, Josh Turner, in which he congratulated me and told me if I had any questions to call him.

I have no idea that on this day, I'll be able to ask these questions in person.

125

PAPER OR PLASTIC?

I know it's a great bit for my hometown visit clip. *Showing Scotty McCreery at Lowes Foods, where he used to be a cashier.* But I love going in there and seeing folks I used to work with and getting an overwhelming greeting. The store manager, Terry Mascaro, gives me an apron to put on and reminds me there's a job waiting for me if I want to come back. The store is mobbed, and it's hard to even walk a few inches. I eventually decide to stand on a conveyor belt at a register just to say hi.

Seeing an entire store full of people and overflowing into the parking lot—it's crazy. I've spent a lot of time on the show posing and smiling for cameras during the last couple of months, but there's absolutely no way to outdo the grin that's stuck on my face now. I feel like the whole town's been given laughing gas, and I'm right in the middle of them all.

I actually ring out some people and have no idea if I'm overcharging them or if they're really even buying whatever things they give me. There are lights, cameras, and lots and lots of action. I see tons of phones staring me down. I work the register and figure they'll tell me when to stop and what to do next.

A fun little thing happens when I'm at Lowes. I jump back up on the counter and try to silence everybody.

"Hey," I say, holding my phone in my hand, "I just got a text from the judges. This is what they said."

Hi, Scotty. The song we've selected for you next week is "She Believes in Me" by Kenny Rogers.

The roar is confirmation they love the choice.
"We gotta do it," I tell them.
It's no *I* gotta do it; it's *we*.

BACK TO SCHOOL

I step out of the sprawling SUV limousine and see all my classmates from Garner High and wave and then hear . . . crickets.

Nah. I get the sort of response I thought I'd get. The grandmothers who love me aren't here. Neither are the sixth graders. These are my friends and the kids I've grown up with. They know me, perhaps *too* well.

"We need to do another take," one of the producers tells us. "The crowd needs to be louder."

I can only laugh. As the limo drives away to make another pass, I wonder if the camera crew is going to toss out donuts and candy bars to all of the students. I step out of the car and hear my name being chanted, and I smile, feeling both proud and silly at the same time. I wave my hands and then do something I've been doing a lot today—clasping my hands over my head and looking down in disbelief.

It's great to see my Garner Magnet High family. The students and the expressions on their faces and the signs they're holding make me understand why I've made it this far. They're one of the many groups that have been behind me the whole time.

It's good to say hi to some of them, even if it's for the briefest of moments.

To walk the hallways once more—

To see the teachers and say hello—

To notice signs on the wall that have my face and name on them—

> On Scotty's hometown visit, he visited his chorus class. After the cameras left, he sat down at the piano and began to pick out a song he learned to play while in LA. All of my students gathered around him, put their arms around each other, and began to sing "Lean on Me" at the top of their lungs as he played. For my teacher heart, it was a priceless moment to watch my students bonding like that and to see Scotty back home with his friends.
>
> MEREDITH CLAYTON,
> CHORUS TEACHER

To go out and throw some pitches with my team—

To see guys and girls my age, doing what I was doing just a few months ago—

They're all reminders of how quickly life can change. And how that doesn't have to change us.

I climb back in the limo, and just before we pull away, a neighbor, Scott Powell, says hi to me.

"We're proud of you," he quietly tells me.

It stuns me a bit. It's the straw that breaks the camel's back. It's not something a guy in high school expects to hear from another guy. When the window shuts, I find myself alone with this overwhelming sense of gratitude and just plain disbelief. I break down and shed a few tears. Thankfully, it's just me in the limo.

Well, me and the cameraman. But I'm used to them by now.

I'm not used to *this*. And I never will be either.

NO MORE IMITATING

It's May 14 and the first time I've been home since February 11. The first time I've ridden on my street, stepped foot onto my driveway, and walked through the doorway to my home. It's nice to be back, even if it's just for a few short moments and memories before getting back to work in Hollywood.

There was a time a few weeks ago when I had a

heart-to-heart talk with Mom. It had been after I reached the Top 5. She knew things were truly serious, and she was thinking about what that meant.

"The Idols *LIVE!* Tour starts right after the show ends in a few weeks," she reminds me, along with everything else.

Basically, Mom was saying there was no longer a question *if* life was about to change for me and for our family. It had already changed.

"It's only May, and we might not be back home until fall."

I wasn't becoming legal anytime soon, so that meant I would still need my legal guardian shadowing my moves. I knew Mom was feeling stressed about everything going on back home. She was running two businesses, plus she needed to check on her mom near the coast and of course plug in with Ashley. Ashley had just started at UNC-Charlotte. Mom was very concerned Ash would feel like a ship without a sail since Dad was traveling around the country with his job at Schneider Electric. I understood when she told me what she needed to do.

"I have to go back to North Carolina for a week," Mom said. "Dad can come out and stay with you for a week. He'll love it. Plus, I think Lauren's dad, J.J., will be here. They'll have a ball."

It would definitely be an interesting experience for Dad, since he was there during Lady Gaga

Week, a memory neither of us will *ever* forget. I think of Mom going back home that week and find myself wishing I could have done the same. There are so many things I'd love to have more time to do. I wish I had not just minutes, but hours. Days.

While visiting my house briefly during the *Idol* visit, I check out my bedroom. I see snapshots of the life I once knew. I don't want to say it's a life I've left behind. I'll never leave this life behind. But things have changed quite a bit, and I am going to be journeying far away for some time.

I pick up that familiar book that helped influence my musical journey. I glance at the cover and smile, and then I open *Be Elvis!* and flip through the worn pages. I have this book practically memorized.

There's no need to imitate Elvis anymore. You don't have to try to be anybody.

America now knows the kid who read about how to talk, sing, perform, and command the stage like Elvis. That was my fascination and love, and one of the reasons I've reached this point.

I'm reminded of the words Priscilla Presley told me: "Elvis would have loved you."

And I think of a quote I once read from Elvis: "I'm trying to keep a level head. You have to be careful out in the world. It's so easy to get turned."

I know I don't have to imitate anybody. I'm doing fine just being myself. Just being Scotty

McCreery, the kid from Garner, North Carolina. As long as I keep a level head and remain careful, I can stay that kid too.

BREAKING ACCUWEATHER REPORT!

Before heading to the parade and the concert in the park, we check the forecast. Channel 5 shows the Dual Doppler 5000 radar. With a name like that, it *has* to be accurate. As we look at the screen, all of us in the family room burst into laughter. Raleigh is pictured, and below it the word *SCOTTY* stands out.

Above us to the north is a red line of severe thunderstorms. Below us to the south is another wave of red, showing more severe thunderstorms. But SCOTTY is in the clear.

I had already mentioned to my pastor, Travis Tobin, about praying for the weather and finding Amos 4:7 when I looked in the Bible for encouragement. He told me the verse is actually a description of judgment on the Israelites for disobeying him.

"But the Bible is a living word, and it can speak to us in many different ways."

I can't help looking at the radar map and thinking back to the verse.

"I also withheld rain."

Thank You, Lord. Thank You.

RIGHT PLACE, RIGHT TIME

"GOOD LUCK, SCOTTY!"

Some store selling signs must've had a "buy one, get a dozen free" sale, since I've seen so many of these in Garner. The theme from *The Lion King* seems to be floating in the air.

"Can You Feel the Love Tonight?"

I sure can. Everywhere I go, I can feel it.

It's a strange thing to wave at a young girl you've never seen and watch her eyes widen and her face suddenly burst into tears. Thankfully, they're the good kind. Those tears have been contagious too. Lots of folks have been seen with a slight case of the sniffles today. I'm one of them.

It's impossible to reflect on everything. The moments are blurry, and I feel like I'm watching a trailer of my own life, with so many smiles, screams, and sensational greetings from everyone.

Mom, Dad, and I are being escorted in a Ford Mustang, saying hello to everybody along Buffaloe Road as we make our way to Lake Benson Park, where the concert is going to be held. The closer we get, the more people we see.

There are the screams. All the folks wearing Scotty McCreery shirts and signs. The young girls smiling, jumping, and dancing. The people cheering and singing. Then there are the boys running, hooting, and hollering. The parents beaming with pride. There's a whole town, and they're staring at *me,* not at some big-name celebrity. Nope.

I think they're all seeing themselves. They're going, *Yeah.* They're thinking, *He's one of us. He's just like me.*

And the truth is that I most certainly am.

The "I Love Scotty" signs, the Scotty McCreery cupcakes, the life-size poster cutouts of me—they may as well all read, "I Love Garner." They may as well be telling America about this small town in North Carolina. Just another town that could be anywhere except . . . Except, no. Our town is special. And everybody watching—at least this is what I think—is feeling the same way. They're thinking, *I know Garner and I can relate to Garner because I live in Garner.* Except their Garner may be in Nebraska or Washington or Maine or Alabama.

I spot a sign held by a girl on the side of the road: "With God All Things Are Possible."

I couldn't say it any better.

As we enter the park and see the rows of friends and fans, the car stops for a moment. A woman comes up to my mother and begins talking to her. I can tell Mom is suddenly becoming more emotional. She's wiping away tears and looking completely overwhelmed.

It turns out this is the daughter of the guy driving our convertible. Stephanie Shaffer works for the park and is sharing some encouraging

> I've won the Garner mayor's race four times. It was surprising, however, after one election to hear Garner residents submitted some write-in votes for another candidate who didn't spend a dime on campaigning. Who was it? Who else? Scotty McCreery.
>
> RONNIE WILLIAMS,
> MAYOR OF GARNER

words. Mom soon brings her over to talk to me. The woman congratulates me and shares how she's been a big fan since day one.

Then she says something I'll never forget.

"God has you right where He wants you to be, Scotty."

I know this and believe it, but hearing it spoken by Stephanie feels like someone handing me a cup of water after I've run a marathon.

I never wondered about what the rest of the world looked like, since I've always been happy with Garner and North Carolina. I've never wished I could've been someone else or been born somewhere else. But suddenly, being here in Garner, being a kid raised here, takes on a whole new meaning.

Our car heads closer to the park, and I can see an endless wave of people. It's just too much.

I think of what America's going to be thinking

when they watch this. When they finally get to see what I've been seeing and knowing my whole life. This is my hometown, these are my people, and this is why I'm here.

Sitting on the back hood of the Mustang between my parents, with so many neighbors, friends, family, and Garner folks surrounding us, I blink and see what this looks like. This crowd, this car, and this kid sitting at the center.

I look up and feel God looking down on me.

Thank You.

I nod, clasp my hands together, and feel overcome with emotion once again.

This moment is not about me. It's just not.

Let me be a mirror, Lord. Let me keep my face looking upward. Let me help others do the same.

My prayer is suddenly put on pause when I see a sweet grandmother holding a "HOTTIE SCOTTY" sign. I just laugh, continue to smile, and hopefully show everyone how thankful I am. How glad I am that they're here with me. Here with America.

I know I'm in the right place today.

Keep me in the right places, Lord. Wherever the roads are gonna lead.

A DUET WITH MY HERO

"There's an election in our county, and I'm glad I don't have to run against this kid," Mayor

Ronnie Williams says into the microphone as thirty thousand people applaud. "Scotty, on behalf of the town of Garner, it's my pleasure to present to you the key to the town."

"What door does it open?" I ask him.

It seems like I've already been given a chestful of keys, ones that have opened millions of doors.

I'm finally onstage in front of the hometown that has made it possible for me to be on this stage. I begin the show by singing "Gone."

As I stand on this stage, there are things I want and need to share, including how much I appreciate everyone here. The first things I tell them are the things that matter.

"Garner, North Carolina, I love you so much. I love you so, so much. I am so thankful—so thankful—to come from such a great town filled with such good people who came to Lake Benson Park today."

Shouts and screams.

"This has been such an incredible journey. God has gotten me through every second of it. I love Him with all my heart. And you guys keep putting me through. So I'm going to try my very best every single week."

I sing a couple more songs, continuing to thank everybody here and telling them how much I appreciate them. Before I sing "Your Man," my theme song on the show, I share what it's been like to be gone for so long.

"I've been away from this town for about four months now. It's been a struggle for me. I've just had my mom out there. My family just comes out there to watch the shows. She's been the only one I can lean on. For me—a lot of people—if you read that tract out there, a lot of you might think since I've been gone and away from my home church that my faith in God might have suffered and kind of dissipated since I've been gone. But it's grown stronger. Each and every day. Each and every day. He's the one I lean on when times get tough. This show is seven days a week. We're working all day long. But anytime I want to throw in the towel, I just lean on Him."

I start the song that got me to this place. Thirty seconds into it, I kneel as I sing the verse, and the crowd suddenly seems to get louder. They must be really feeling it. I'm thinking I've got them in the palm of my hand. I stand and move around the stage, and as I turn, I see someone approaching and I'm about to put my arm around whomever it might be.

"Oh my God," I shout as I reel back in complete disbelief. "Oh my goodness."

Josh Turner is standing there with a big ole grin on his face. They got me. I honestly had no idea he'd be here. None.

I hand him the mic and tell him to sing 'cause I don't even realize he's holding one in his hands. He puts an arm around me and then shakes my hand.

"Scotty McCreery, everybody," Josh tells the crowd.

"Josh Turner, the man," I say, shaking my head and bending over a bit to try to wrap my head around all this.

No way.

The song stops, and the cheering grows more intense. Josh extends his arm to the crowd.

"All these people are here for you," he says.

I extend my arm as well. "This is Garner, North Carolina. I'm telling you. Aren't they great?"

The music begins again. The show must go on.

"Give it up for Mr. Josh Turner, ladies and gentlemen."

There are moments in life when you have to go big or go home. You have to stand up and acknowledge the utter insanity of the moment and go, *Yeah, I'm here, I'm doing this, it's time. Go sing along with your idol*—so you do.

You might have to pause and look back at the band and say, "Whoa"—but you have to regain your focus. There's a whole town of folks out there in front of you.

Actually, there are more people here than live in our whole town.

They've just had another privilege of seeing one of my heroes—one of theirs as well—visiting our small town to join me in singing his song.

Most of the world saw me surprise Scotty on *American Idol* in his hometown of Garner, North Carolina. What most of the world didn't see were the sold-out hotels, the messages on business signs, the messages written on car windows, the signs in people's yards, the young girls in front of the stage crying in hysterics when he came close to them, and the thirty-thousand-plus people who turned out for him to do five songs or so! It was the closest thing to Beatlemania I've ever witnessed. What I loved most about it is that he's a good Christian guy who has his head screwed on straight.

JOSH TURNER

"Aren't y'all glad you came out tonight?" I tell the crowd. "Forget about me—look at this man right here."

Ever the gracious and humble singer, Josh tells me how everybody in Garner and all over North Carolina are so proud of me, including himself.

"Thank you for singing my songs," Josh tells me with a chuckle.

"Thank *you* for singing them."

Josh says he can't leave without singing the

song that got him to where he's at now. I have to add that it's my personal favorite song. As he gets his guitar ready, Josh talks about growing up idolizing Randy Travis, a singer who grew up in North Carolina not too far from us.

"There's something in the water down around this area of the Carolinas," Josh says.

"This man here—he's been my hero," I say about Josh. "Honestly. The way he lives his life as a Christian man in Nashville around all the songs out there talking about drinking and every thing—this man stays clean. And I respect him more than anything out there."

That tough, textured voice launches into "Long Black Train." Soon we're singing together.

"Victory in the Lord."

Amen.

W

For a few moments—or maybe it's hours—I break down after singing the last song from my set. It's the song I first performed at "Clayton Idol," the one that launched the idea and the belief that I could do such a thing like this.

When I sing those last two words—"in color"— a waterfall of emotion pours out of me. I'm alone on the stage and hear the applause and see the enthusiasm, and I can't say anything. Tears come, and I try to regain my composure.

Come on, Scotty. You've been singing in front

of America for the past three months. You can do this.

But I can't. I don't know what to say.

That's when I look and see my parents and Ashley coming to my side. For a moment, it's just the four of us. It doesn't matter where we are or who's watching. I'm reminded of how much I love and need these other three people. How much they've done for me and are continuing to do, even at this very moment.

I hug my family and feel this wave of love about to come out of me. The kind you wonder where it came from and how you deserve it. The tears are flowing.

"I'm so proud of you," Mom says as I embrace her. "God is so proud of you too."

My father puts his hands on my shoulders from behind, like a coach might do to his quarterback who just won the game for them.

"You witnessed to a lot of people today. Awesome job, son."

I know something at this very moment.

This—*this* right now—is my winning moment. I don't need a countdown or Ryan Seacrest announcing my name. I don't need lights, commercial breaks, or balloons and confetti falling down on my head.

Mom, Dad, and Ashley are here. So is the rest of my hometown. They've all witnessed my dreams suddenly being fulfilled, along with the encouragement to go out and run with them.

It's enough. It's more than enough.

This right here—this is what victory looks like.

With God all things are possible.

Yes, they are.

"I love y'all so much," I tell all my friends in my hometown one more time.

I just have to add one more little thing.

"This is Top 3. And I'm going to work my tail off to win this thing and bring it back to Garner, North Carolina."

I've already won. Now it's time to bring the W home to all of them.

Shortly after I walk off the stage, the skies open up, and it starts to pour. Really.

Chapter Six

Hollywood
and Homework

I watch the YouTube video one more time. It shows Ryan Seacrest announcing the winner of Season 10 of *American Idol*, but that's not why I'm watching it over and over. The video resembles a hockey game more than it does the last few minutes of a reality show. You have to squint to see Lauren and me on the screens hanging from the ceiling of the PNC Arena in Raleigh, North Carolina. The images that fill up most of the YouTube video are the thousands of people inside the arena, watching the screens at the *Idol* viewing party held in Raleigh on finale night. The final *Idol* viewing party they'll be having. What started out with just thirty or forty folks now numbers into the thousands.

When my name is announced, the place erupts into pandemonium.

More than twenty-nine million people are said to be watching this year's finale. But the people standing up, screaming, and celebrating in the PNC Arena are some of the most important ones. It's cool to be able to watch them cheering me on, even if it's a day or two after winning *Idol*.

ANIMAL CRACKERS

"Sing for the laughter, sing for the tear."

I still remember Steven Tyler performing "Dream On" at the finale just before the announcement was made. How could I have sung more songs that night than he did?

The words of that song seem to be an appropriate summary of this whole musical journey. It also seems to foreshadow the months and years to come.

It's impossible to reflect on what's happening finale night. Like the entire season, I'm too busy to actually have any perspective. Getting a chance to share my story with you allows me an opportunity to reflect on it myself.

I just remember a few things standing out about that night.

I'm able to sing "Live Like You Were Dying" with Tim McGraw. This is the song I chose for my first guitar solo when I started lessons at age nine, sung by a hero of mine I'd grown up listening to. As we rehearsed together for the first time, Tim could tell I was nervous, so he gave me some incredible encouragement.

"Listen, Scotty, this is your show, not mine. Just be yourself and don't worry about anything."

There were all the performances. The bold and bright Beyoncé. Jennifer Lopez bringing some Latin vibes to the evening by performing a salsa while Marc Anthony sang alongside her. The performance by Lady Gaga, which is—well, it's pretty interesting for a family show.

Before the show, the producers tell me I can have anything I want in my dressing room. This is the big night, and I can get *whatever I want*. It'll be my first true introduction to the legendary tour rider—documents that list the things an artist wants while touring. Over the years, these have become more and more outrageous.

So here's my chance:

- an all-you-can-eat Bojangles' buffet and lots of sweet tea
- posters of Elvis and Cash performing
- a television playing the highlights of the New England Patriots Super Bowls won in 2001, 2003, and 2004
- the soundtrack to Rocky playing in the background
- egg salad with no mayo and must not have an egg taste accompanying it
- M&Ms (WARNING: ABSOLUTELY NO BROWN ONES)

But you know, after coming this far and being here on finale night, I can really only think of one thing I'd like to have.

"How 'bout some animal crackers?"

For some reason, the last four weeks, I've just been craving them.

If the producers didn't already know me, they'd probably be thinking, *Who is this guy?*

They know I'm a simple guy. Really. It's no act. And right now, all I really want is some animal crackers. I haven't had any in a while.

After they leave to get me some, I wonder if I should have played the artist card. Just a little.

"Animal crackers," I could have said, "but *absolutely NO elephants.*"

Yeah. Maybe I'll wait to make those sorts of demands. Or at least until after I see whether or not I win tonight.

FORD FUN

On the night of the finale, I discover one of the great loves of my life. Her name begins with an "L."

Oh, come on now. I know what you're thinking.

I'm talking about Loretta, the Ford truck I win if I win the competition.

Every Sunday during our *Idol* season, the finalists spend the day working on a new Ford commercial. Doing this was a blast. One week we would be working on what looked like a massive art project, designing our own stage. Another Sunday would find us acting out movie roles and later watching the same characters at a drive-in theater.

The most fun we had was filming the "Zombie

Picnic" commercial for the Top 8. Never did I imagine I'd get to be on television playing the role of an undead person. A sharply dressed undead person, mind you. At first glance, it looks like I'm heading straight toward Lauren to attack her, but then I change my mind. All of the zombies get into the Mustang and then start jammin' out to the song.

We get to spend a lot of time inside and around Ford vehicles. There are even two Ford Mustangs that stay parked at the mansion, reminding us that whoever wins the competition may well get to drive one of them back home. All of us knew that previous *Idol* winners had won Ford cars.

But you guessed it. I wanted a truck. It would sure be cool to replace my beat-up 4Runner back home.

The best thing Ford does that whole season is to bring Ms. Clayton to the finale. Meredith Covington Clayton is my classical choral director at Garner High. I was in her advanced classical choral group called Die Meistersingers. Every day of high school, I spent an hour and a half in her fine arts class studying classical music and performance technique. I've been working with her since I was a freshman, so it makes sense to pick her as the schoolteacher who impacted me the most.

During my hometown visit, I'm able to visit Ms. Clayton and the chorus at my high school.

She taught me so much about singing and performing, and for a long time she did this without knowing my love for country music or the low twang in my voice. Believe it or not, when I first started in her choral program, she actually put me with the tenors. As my voice began to drop—or more like plummet—I had to go to her and ask to be put in the bass section.

So Ford allows us to invite our chosen special teacher to the finale. Lauren Alaina invites her principal, while I chose Ms. Clayton. They both look lovely, all dressed up for the big event. Off camera, Ryan looks at me and says, "Your teacher's a fox!"

Both Lauren and I get to deliver special news to them on live TV.

"Here are the keys to your brand-new Ford Focus," we say in unison.

It's pretty incredible to give someone you respect a car that you didn't even pay for. There are smiles, hugs, applause, and genuine surprise. Then Ryan shares more news with Lauren and me—news we were expecting, but not exactly *this* kind of news.

"By the way," he says, "Ford has a surprise for both of you—the keys to *any Ford vehicle you want.*"

Suddenly the show and the competition and the packed auditorium all go away as I have one thought in my head.

F-250.

On my first album released just over four months later, there'll be a fun song called "You Make That Look Good." The opening lyrics go like this:

"I'm just a country boy, I drive a four-by-four."

After *Idol*, I actually do get the chance to test-drive that souped-up and decked-out Ford F-250 truck. Now, if you're not into trucks and have never seen one of these, it's a beast. My mom was there with me for the test-drive, and she called it a Sherman tank, the massive kind used in World War II. The truck is awesome, but it's also a bit like driving a small semi.

"This is never going to fit in our garage," Mom tells me.

I usually go big or go home, but in this case, I decided not to go *that* big. The F-150 King Ranch ends up being big enough for me. I name it Loretta.

Since I'm on the road so much, days and weeks can pass when I don't get to see Loretta. When I'm home, however, I treat Loretta right. I've given her all sorts of gifts—tinted windows, a leveling kit, decals, and big ole tires.

I'll be honest, though. I haven't always treated Loretta right. Every single window has either been scratched or broken. One night, I landed at the Raleigh-Durham airport late. It was winter, and North Carolina had one of its famous ice storms while Loretta sat in the airport parking lot for several days. I jogged out to Loretta, only to find every window coated with thick ice. It took me five minutes to get the door open. I found something in my book bag that looked like it could break ice and spent what seemed like thirty minutes busting ice. The next morning in the daylight, I see I've cracked or scratched every window on Loretta. Yep—I would end up having to get every window replaced. There have also been a few dents and lots and lots of dirty drives.

All inspiration for a good song.

"It's usually covered in mud, from the axle to the door. It's a little banged-up, a little too much rust."

Once while I was driving around a shopping center in Raleigh, an elderly man drove right into Loretta. The repair bill cost me almost a grand. I decided to pay for it, however. He was a nice guy. I didn't want to call the cops on him.

I knew good ole Loretta could handle it.

Thank you, Ford, for setting the two of us up.

"I'M GOING TO GARNER!"

Nobody knows I'm back home.

Some people who win big competitions and become voted the most valuable player end up getting a chance to go to Disneyland. And I'll actually be at Disney World in a few days. But first, I get the great opportunity to come back to Garner to . . . *take an AP English test?*

Somehow this whole "living the dream" thing hasn't exactly happened just yet.

It's after midnight, and I arrive at the Raleigh-Durham airport, along with a security guard from *Idol* named Sal. It's been a little over twenty-four hours since the finale. After my victory was a long night of celebrations, interviews, meetings, and parties. I may have slept a few hours before waking up at 4:00 a.m. the next morning to start a full day of interviews. Now we're being picked up by Dad in my old Toyota 4Runner.

"You want to drive?" Dad asks when he sees me at the baggage claim. He knows I haven't driven in months.

I tell him sure, but it's only when we get into Garner that Dad remembers I wanted to drive. He pulls up to a stop sign on Aversboro Road, and we do a Chinese fire drill, switching seats quickly. It's nice to be behind the wheel. Yes, it's not a Ford 250 or 150, but it's my vehicle. It feels normal. Few things in the last three months have felt normal.

You're not going to believe this, but I swear it happens. Ten seconds, maybe fifteen, after I start driving my car, a song comes on the radio.

Yep.

My first single, "I Love You This Big," begins to play on WQDR. We all start screaming. Sal the

> On a rainy night in Vancouver, I watched *American Idol* for the first time. The song "Swingin' " blew me away! "Wow, who is that kid? That kid is fantastic." Since that night, I've traveled up to eight hours to see Scotty sing. Going to at least twenty-five concerts, I met his whole family, lots of lovely fans, and even became friends with his tour bus on Twitter, ha ha! But what I discovered most was Scotty himself—a kid with an incredible voice and, even more importantly, a great human being with a heart big enough to reach all the way to Canada and beyond.
>
> LOUISE LEMIEUX,
> McCREERIAN FROM
> VANCOUVER, BRITISH COLUMBIA

security guard is surely thinking we're all crazy, but we explain this is the first time any of us have heard the song on the radio.

I just laugh, shake my head, and think, *Hey—that's me.*

It's pretty cool. I left Garner last February to give *Idol* a shot. Three months later, I'm home, driving around and listening to myself on the radio. Times have changed.

It's like God pressed a button on His playlist just to remind me He's thinking about me.

The next day, I'm in a room taking the three-hour AP English test. This might seem crazy—well, it kinda is—but I'm not simply walking away from school. I've talked about this plenty with my parents. They are fine either way—this was my decision. I'm going to go back for my senior year and try to go to college. I can figure out later what that means with the music and the touring and all that. We can deal with those decisions when the time comes.

For now, I just have to do my best on this test.

Too bad I can't get people to call in and help me out on this.

"THIS BIG"

We actually had forgotten that the song we heard on the radio and freaked out about while driving in Garner had been released. And not to toot my own horn, but I do want to share some cool things about my first single. In some ways, that song is from another era of music. Before the world of streaming and Spotify took over our industry. It might be something I never see again in my life-time, even if I end up having numerous number ones to celebrate.

"I Love You This Big" releases right after the *Idol* finale on May 25. It ends up debuting at #32 on the *Billboard* Country Songs chart, making it the highest debut for a brand-new artist since they began tracking those numbers in 1990. It sells 171,404 units that first week. It ends up reaching #11 on the *Billboard* Hot 100 and becomes a Top 15 radio hit. By August, it achieves certified gold status (meaning half a million have been sold). It'll eventually reach platinum status.

This is all happening, and I'm not even legal.

I can't take credit for these things. Yes, I can say, like so many artists do, that I need to thank God—and I certainly do. But I also have to thank the huge team at *American Idol*, the radio promo team at my label, and especially country radio. There are the songwriters—Lil' Ronnie, Ester Dean, and Brett James. They wrote the right song with the right lyrics to connect with my moment at the end of *Idol* and to also connect with all my fans.

What a way to start, right? So incredible.

Even more incredible is being able to sing this song for groups like the kids at Disney's Hollywood Studios at Disney World not long after winning *Idol*. I'm able to share with them my thoughts and feelings on my debut single.

"I fell in love with this song when I heard it," I say. "This song can be interpreted in so many different ways. You can think of it in terms of a man saying to his woman, 'I love you this big, honey.' Or you can talk about it in terms of a little kid saying to her parent, 'I love you this big, Mom.' Or you can talk about it in terms of my Lord and Savior Jesus Christ when He was on the cross—how He spread His arms wide open, saying, 'I love you that big.' "

That's the sort of big I'll never be able to fully understand. But singing about it helps me remember it.

LIVE WITH REGIS AND SCOTTY!

"You remind me of Opie," Regis Philbin tells me.

Well, I guess there are worse people to be compared to.

"Maybe you should be Opie, and I can be Andy Griffith," he says.

You gotta love Regis Philbin. I'm making the rounds doing shows, and I'm on *Live with Regis and Kelly*. It's a fun interview, like so many of them are. People tend to ask some of the same things, but I get an interesting question to start out with today.

"Is there something you're not good at?" Kelly Ripa wants to know. "Give us the number one thing you're bad at."

"Soccer," I say without hesitation. "I tried out for my soccer team and got cut the first day. The coach felt bad for me 'cause all my buddies made the team. So I was kind of the manager/assistant coach. During the season, if they didn't call me 'coach,' they ran a lap."

I'm growing used to being in front of people on live television to do these interviews. Interviewers love mentioning the fact that I worked at a grocery store. I'm asked about the famous Steven Tyler moment. I'm asked about the singers I grew up loving. I'm even asked to do an Elvis impersona-tion.

"Well, it's one for the money," I sing from "Blue Suede Shoes."

The cool thing is that every time I do one of these interviews, there are thousands of people who've never heard any of this. We live in a busy world full of lots of people saying and doing lots of different things. Sure, almost thirty million people watched the *Idol* finale, but more than three hundred million people live in the United States! I've met so many people who never watched a single episode of *Idol*. It's okay. To be able to share a little about myself and my voice—I love it.

CMA MUSIC FESTIVAL 2011

It's not really cool for guys to talk in the restroom. At least not as far as I'm concerned. So meeting Keith Urban in the bathroom during the CMT Awards isn't the top place I would've picked for running into one of my musical heroes.

I had heard someone in the restroom singing, and all I could think was, *Who is that cat?* Then suddenly out walks the man himself. The coolest

Scotty asked me to sit with him at the 2011 CMA Awards show in his one allowed guest seat. When Scotty and I were escorted to our seats, we saw all the big stars sitting around us. We were both pretty star-struck. It was an incredible night getting to watch my little brother live out his dream at one of country music's biggest shows.

ASHLEY McCREERY

thing about this is Keith instantly says hi to me before I can greet him.

"Scotty, how's it going?"

I never thought guys like Keith would know me by name, and it still blows me away.

"Hey" is all I really manage to say. We wash and dry our hands, then shake hands, and head back out to the awards show. There are a million questions I could have asked that man, but the men's restroom wasn't the place or the time.

Who could have guessed Keith Urban and I would have two common bonds? He would find his place on *Idol* as a judge, and I would put one of his early songs—"Walk in the Country"—on my first album.

This will be one of many memories made during the CMA Music Festival week in Nashville that June.

Lauren and I are introduced by fellow *Idol* winner Carrie Underwood that Tuesday night at the Grand Ole Opry. It's announced that we'll be making our debut performances this Friday. The CMT Music Awards are on Wednesday, and then we're signing autographs in downtown Nashville before we sing later at the Opry. We will be able to participate in the City of Hope Softball Challenge on Saturday and then make it all the way to the main stage at LP Field that night. I'll be singing with Josh Turner, while Lauren is singing with Martina McBride.

I'm hearing and saying the word *debut* a lot. Talking about my age a lot. Saying a lot of the same things over and over. How it's all unexpected, how it's been so cool, how it's been quite a trip.

"I'm playing for seventy thousand people tonight," I say about getting on the stage at LP Field. "I never dreamed of that."

Dreams are strange things. It's rare when you finally stop and see yourself and then put your hands up and realize the dream has arrived.

Uh, you know, Scotty—Ryan did that for you moments after you won.

Yeah, well, still. In the busy moments of living out those dreams—meeting fans, singing, performing, and running into *your* idols—it's hard to stop and find yourself being proud of where you're at. Not prideful. I'm talking more about a gracious and humbling place.

Like I said after winning *Idol*, I have to thank the Lord first for getting me here.

LOTS OF LOVE

There are other things to be focused on besides doing interviews, jumping up on stages to sing, or being at music-related events.

I've got an album to make.

No pressure, except for the fact I have *forty-nine upcoming shows* across the United States, Canada, and the Philippines for the Idols *LIVE!* Tour.

The American Idols *LIVE!* Tour 2011 is set to begin on July 6, but rehearsals will be coming much sooner than that. The tour ends in mid-September. And somehow, I'm supposed to find time to record more songs to go on my debut album. The label wants to release it *yesterday*.

During CMA Music Festival Week in Nashville, I go to the studio to work with the guy who's going to produce my album. His name is Mark Bright. I first met Mark in LA during *Idol*. He had been asked to come out to work with me during Top 3 Week. It made sense since he'd worked with Rascal Flatts and Carrie Underwood and had tremendous success. Our first few times together went great, so I was thrilled to be working with him on the new album.

I meet with Mark and his team at Starstruck

Studios in Nashville. Its name fits. The place is owned by Reba McEntire, and all the big artists have recorded here. When I arrive on that first day, Mark introduces me to the studio musicians who work with him. Now these guys are true artists.

One of them is a pianist named Gordon Mote. Talk about an inspiration. I find out Gordon has been blind since birth, yet he grew up grounded by his faith and dreaming of doing something with his passion in music. He's from Alabama and grew up traveling and singing in churches of all kinds.

Two days after Gordon graduated from Belmont University with honors, Lee Greenwood asked him to join his band. *Two days.* That's how good Gordon is. He's toured with a variety of artists, including Trisha Yearwood and the Gaither Vocal Band.

His big break came when he filled in for a keyboardist at a recording session. It just so happened that Alan Jackson was cutting "Where Were You (When the World Stopped Turning)", the same number one hit I sang during *Idol*. Since then, Gordon has played for all the big names out there. But he also has a bunch of vocal and instrumental albums of his own.

The drummer I shake hands with is Paul Leim, and it would take a whole chapter to list all his credits. He's managed to use his talent on the drums not only on records but also in movies, television shows, and live performances. His many album credits include Dolly Parton, Tanya Tucker, Randy Travis, Kenny Rogers, and Lionel Richie. He worked with John Williams on the music for *Return of the Jedi*. He's performed on shows like *The Tonight Show*. Paul's done all this while being a husband and father of three kids.

Another legendary guy I meet is a session guitarist named Brent Mason. He's been in the studio with Alan Jackson, Brooks & Dunn, George Strait, Shania Twain, and Neil Diamond. He's won a Grammy and two CMA awards. His experience and his mastery on the guitar are incredible.

These guys are all going to be recording. *With me.*

As I meet all these guys, a little piece of home calms my nerves a bit. Derek Bason, Mark's engineer who always works with him, is from North Carolina and is wearing a UNC Tar Heels shirt. It's not accidental either. They know I'm a big NC State Wolfpack fan. We instantly start the banter that Wolfpack and Tar Heels fans always have.

It feels good having a little North Carolina here with me in Nashville.

After the introductions, Mark Bright does something I haven't seen so far in any sessions I've had.

"I just think we should pray before we start recording," Mark says.

It's unusual, and so very right to do. What I discover recording with these guys is that there's lots of love, encouragement, and joy in the process.

"Let 'er rip, tater," Mark says when it's my time to sing. He'll say it a lot, since we lay down five songs that very first day.

None of us know that this album—*Clear as Day*—we're working on will set a couple of *Billboard* records and take only thirteen weeks to go platinum. In October 2011, *Clear as Day* debuted at no. 1 on the *Billboard* Top 200, at that time making me the first country artist, as well as the youngest male artist, to do so with their first studio album. *Clear as Day* reached no. 1 on five separate *Billboard* charts—*Billboard* 200, Top Current Albums, Digital Albums, Internet Albums, and Top Country Albums. It would be one of the highest-selling *American Idol* debuts of all time, moving one million copies in just three months.

Even if those guys had known it, they probably wouldn't have cared. They're pros, and the numbers and accolades aren't why they're doing this. They're doing the thing they love to do, and as a bonus they're getting paid to do it.

THE IDOLS *LIVE!* TOUR

As I mentioned, the Top 11 contestants from our *Idol* season head out to perform forty-nine shows. It might be one of the last times an Idols *LIVE!* Tour is this massive. This season's tour is the first time eleven finalists participate instead of ten. This tour is also only the second time it has traveled to Asia. The tour's response is overwhelming and almost a complete sellout.

We've been together for months, but we still all get along. There's nobody wearing the number representing their final position in *Idol*. Certainly there's more of a focus on Lauren and me since we were the top two finalists. The show itself has more ensemble performances than years past, with songs from artists ranging from Maroon 5 and Katy Perry to Guns N' Roses and Journey. Of course I get to have my Josh Turner and Montgomery Gentry songs in there, along with my own recently released song.

A typical day will look like this: We leave a venue around eleven at night and sleep in our two buses. Mom breathes a sigh of relief when she's told she can stay on the girls' bus. That way she can hang with Lauren's mom, Kristy, and Thia's mom, Cynthia. We arrive at our hotels around four or five in the morning. We check in and get more rest until 11:00 a.m. or so.

From there we go to the next venue, have lunch, do press, and then do rehearsals for the night. Starting around three or so, we have two different meet-and-greet sessions. Then we have dinner, and the show starts after 7:00 p.m.

All of us on the tour are getting a crash course in touring. We're learning things in three months that it takes other musicians *years* to learn. At times it's grueling, always being on the go, living on a bus, and being "together" quite a bit, but it's also the best sort of education a singer can get. The hotels they put us in are nice, and the catering is fabulous. We get to see things like hundreds of enthusiastic fans waiting by the buses after the show to see their favorite musicians and get auto-graphs or pictures with them. We're still riding this crazy *Idol* wave. We love it and enjoy seeing these excited people.

Mom is great to be with because she always takes an active role in helping out with any-thing. We'd have the VIP meet and greet, and sometimes the lines got very long, especially since the fans would be able to go to whichever idol they wanted to meet. Mom would work with Ray, the Idol Tour's security guard, to keep the lines moving, help take pictures, and just make general conver-sation with fans. Folks recognized her since she was visible during the show. She was surprised that many people asked to have a picture with her as well. All of us learned what it was like to truly meet-and-greet and keep things moving and on schedule.

One of the best things about the tour is that I don't have to go onstage until later in the evening. They have sixteen songs before the intermission, and I'm not in any of them. So I do have some free time.

That's why I earn the nickname MIA. The tour managers often find themselves sweating half an hour before I'm supposed to be onstage simply because they can't find me. I am, as they say, "missing in action." Then I'll come walking in the back door, wearing shorts and flip-flops and carrying a souvenir baseball cup in my hand or maybe a pizza. I could catch a good four or five innings before I needed to be onstage.

Yeah, I can admit to that now.

I can also admit to loving my sleep. One late morning around our normal time to leave for the venue, the buses are about to take off, and they're waiting for me. We are in Houston, and the tour manager asks my mom to get off her bus.

"Everyone's on the buses except Scotty," she says. "We need to get going. You two will have to take a cab to the venue."

When I eventually step foot in the hotel lobby, my mom is waiting there with what's known in our family as "the stink eye." And yes, we take a long, quiet cab ride to the venue.

First and last time *that* happens.

Well, maybe not the last. There's the time in 2013 in Virginia while opening for Brad Paisley when my crowded bus leaves me. I was on the phone while my band assumed I was on the bus. I see my bus rolling away from the venue, and I have to run after it, waving my box of Crunch Berries.

I'm able to continue recording my album while on the road. One memorable experience is going to a small place called Dead Aunt Thelma's Studio while we were in Portland, Oregon. All Mark said I needed while there was his special mic, which he would FedEx to the studio. Mark and Derek, his sound engineer, would fly in, and we'd be ready to record. This might not have been the most ideal way to make my first album, but we needed to ride the *Idol* wave and release this album as quickly as possible.

Near the end of the tour, we have two performances in the Philippines. We're really given the whole Beatlemania treatment there. It's crazy because you'll find *American Idol* being shown all day on television. Everybody knows us and goes crazy. An appearance at a mall has fans congregated all around us and staring down from multiple floors above. I know I've used the word *surreal* a lot, but it's a good description for the way this life continues to be.

Speaking of surreal, we end up onstage with world champion boxer Manny Pacquiao. Yes, just

> September 17 and 21, 2011—days I will never forget! "American Idols *LIVE!*" in Manila, Philippines. The days I'd see Scotty McCreery perform live, which I thought would never happen. Scotty has changed my life completely. His music and personality have enlightened me. I've made friends with people across the globe who became family to me because of him. I really am grateful to him and his family. Proud to call myself a McCreerian!
>
> EVITA DESCULA,
> McCREERIAN FROM MANILA, PHILIPPINES

another night in our lives. Manny also does a little singing. We play fight a little, and he gives us autographed jackets. Life is good, even halfway 'round the world.

MEANWHILE, BACK IN MY OTHER LIFE

"Man, I hope this works," I say out loud as I walk to the principal's office.

Garner High School has been in session for a couple of weeks now, but this is my first day back. In a weird way, I feel like it's my first day of school. Ever. I'm still that same kid who walked the halls seven months ago. I even deliberately look like him, with my buzzed haircut, gym shorts, and an old T-shirt. But, man, who can believe what's happened over the last year? Winning *Idol*. Traveling the United States. Recording an album.

I can hear my flip-flops flopping as I walk toward the side door of the high school. The principal, Drew Cook, said to come during second period to avoid any big commotion that morning.

Some industry professionals said it would be impossible—going back to high school to finish my senior year. I disagreed and made it clear I wanted to finish my senior year and try heading to college, but right now I'm not so sure about all this. I only need to pass Senior English to get my diploma, but I really want one more baseball season and to do things like go to homecoming and prom. When I went to Milwaukee, I didn't intend on checking out of the real world at age sixteen.

When I get to Principal Cook's office, I'm greeted by him, as well as a Garner police officer and a Wake County public schools security professional.

Principal Cook tells me his plan for getting me reacclimated into school. He's made an announcement that Scotty's back so let's keep this low-key and please no photographs or pictures—which is a big relief for me. I don't want to stand out any more than I do. Of course, the police officers who accompany me to classes—one on my right and the other on my left—stand out just a bit, I guess.

It's cool, though. After a few days without any drama, my security detail is relieved of their duty. Everybody's handling the situation well, treating me like regular Scotty and acting normal. I know I'll never go back to having a 100 percent normal life, but I can still just be me.

I have a light load my senior year. I had already taken most of my college prerequisites. Later in the year, while touring with Brad Paisley, I document everything, and the school counts it as work study. When I'm on the road touring and doing promotions, I can attend school Monday through Wednesday and then do the musical stuff Thurs-day through Sunday. I can always take school-work with me and make up tests when I'm back. Sometimes I might be cramming on a flight home so I can be ready for school on Monday, but I can do it.

They say youth is wasted on the young, but it's not gonna be wasted on me.

I've checked my touring schedule, and it looks like I'll be able to play baseball too. The coach reminds me of how *normal* I happen to be.

"You gotta get back in shape if you want to play, McCreery," Coach Goffena tells me.

It feels good to be treated like any other player.

FLOWERS ON THE WALL

"Come on, Mom. We can climb over it."

We're in New Orleans for the Idols *LIVE!* Tour, and I want to escape for a while. I've spotted a nearby baseball stadium, so I decide to check it out. This time, Mom is tagging along. Well, at least she was planning to until we reach the four-foot-high concrete barrier behind the Lakefront Arena where we're performing.

"I can't climb that," she says in both humor and disbelief.

"Aw, come on."

I climb it first and then help Mom do the same. I'm thankful neither of us break our necks and get rushed to the ER.

We eventually find ourselves walking on a track that leads to a university baseball field with a game in progress. The park is Maestri Field, which is the home field of the University of New Orleans Privateers. We walk up to the bleachers and blend in. I'm wearing my camo hat and go completely unnoticed.

I gotta admit—it feels great. Just sitting here watching the players on the field. Hearing that familiar sound of the baseball hitting the glove. The crack of the bat. The runner diving toward the base. We watch for a couple innings.

Two innings that remind me of home.

The sun is setting and the hot day is beginning

to cool, and I think about my mother at my side. I might be grateful for this brief respite and for the game I'm watching. But more than anything else, I appreciate Mom for being by my side for so long. Who could have dreamed when we left for Los Angeles last February to start the live show that we'd be gone for many, many months.

My future might find me going to lots of different places on my own, but I know Mom is not going anywhere. She'll always be by my side, ready to climb over a stone wall to stay with me.

My late granddad,
Trooper R. P. Cooke
of the North Carolina
Highway Patrol.

My grandparents
—Bill and Paquita
McCreery—on their
wedding day in
August 1957
in San Juan,
Puerto Rico.

Christmas 2002, age nine—receiving my very first guitar from my granddad R.P. and my grandma Janet.

My first trip to Puerto Rico to visit my grandmother Paquita's native San Juan. As a child, she played at these castles built on the ocean.

In First Baptist Garner's large music ministry, kids as young as three years old begin singing on stage and can be in musicals once they enter elementary school. In fifth grade, I was Joseph in the Christmas play and sang "O Holy Night," one of my favorite carols. I later sang it on my 2012 *Christmas with Scotty* CD.
Ken Hall Photography

Garner High's student section is known as "The Blue Crew." Loved being part of a group with so much spirit. My touring company, "Blue Crew Productions," is named for them. *Ken Hall Photography*

During my sophomore year at Garner High, my classmates talked me into trying out for the lead role of Conrad Birdie in *Bye Bye Birdie.* It was a blast. But baseball season was going on at the same time, and my coach didn't seem too excited about me missing practice.
Ken Hall Photography

This photo was taken in Milwaukee moments after I received my very first golden ticket. Little did we know how the next year would unfold.

Here, I find a quiet spot to study my song during *American Idol*'s Hollywood Week. We were given CDs to help us learn the lyrics and melody. You can see the CD player resting on my leg.

The day of my *American Idol* homecoming visit—May 14, 2011. Thirty thousand people showed up at Lake Benson Park to cheer me on. Storms loomed nearby, but the rain held off until I left the stage.
Raleigh News & Observer

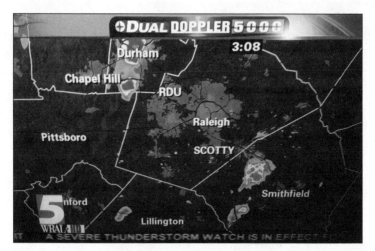

Dual Doppler 5000 radar from WRAL on May 14, 2011, showing storms all around my upcoming *American Idol* homecoming concert in southern Wake County. Moments after the concert ended, the skies opened up and rain poured down. *WRAL*

Admirers along the parade route greet me at the homecoming parade. *Raleigh News & Observer*

Crowds of all ages lined the driveway into Lake Benson Park to greet the parade. *Raleigh News & Observer*

Josh Turner, singer of "Your Man," totally surprised me when he appeared onstage at my homecoming visit. I should have suspected something, because as I prepared for the Garner visit, one of the *Idol* producers told me I absolutely had to perform "Your Man." Josh and I later became friends.
Raleigh News & Observer

My family alongside the stage—mom Judy, aunt Barbara, sister Ashley, and dad Mike— as I performed at Lake Benson Park during the *Idol* homecoming visit in May 2011. *Rob Smith*

Early morning after I won *American Idol*. Tony, my security guard, does his best photo bomb as I catch a quick catnap following 5:30 a.m. press.

The book *Shades of Elvis*, coauthored by Priscilla Presley and Christopher Ameruoso, featured seventy-five celebrities wearing Elvis's actual sunglasses. It was incredible being a part of this project.
Christopher Ameruoso, from the book Shades of Elvis

Following the Idols *LIVE!* Tour show in Charlotte, North Carolina, in July 2011, my sister's coworkers from the NC Baptist Assembly at Camp Caswell do a quick prayer huddle before I leave on the tour bus for the next city.

September 10, 2011. Last night of the U.S. run of the
summer Idols *LIVE!* Tour in Rochester, New York.
Horsing around with James, Paul, and Casey. It's
been a long summer. We get a quick break before we
head out to the Philippines later that month.

The Idols *LIVE!* Tour ended in late September
with two shows in the Philippines. While there,
we did quite a bit of promo on TV and in
huge malls. The response was incredible.

Love my Wolfpack and proud to be part of the NC State family. Had the opportunity to sing the national anthem here prior to a football game in October 2011. *Raleigh News & Observer*

About fifteen thousand people attended my eighteenth birthday party concert at Walnut Creek Amphitheatre in Raleigh in October 2011. I received my first gold album here and did a free concert and Q&A session for fans. *Ken Hall Photography*

Beverly Keel, UMG Nashville's senior vice president at the time, and me on the field in St. Louis before I sang the national anthem for game 1 of the World Series in October 2011. Interesting side note: Beverly's late father, Pinckney Keel—a journalist—covered Elvis at one time and coined the phrase "Elvis the Pelvis."
Beverly Keel

In 2011, I had the opportunity to take part in a shoebox delivery to the Dominican Republic with Operation Christmas Child.

Just had to post this photo from late 2011 when my tour manager, Mike Childers, first started with me. In 2011, he had black hair. Now he's totally gray. Sorry, Mike! *Ken Hall Photography*

American Idol had a great partnership with Disney. Here, I'm singing in the 2011 Disney Parade, which aired on Christmas Day. I also loved to surprise guests at the *American Idol* Experience at Disney's Hollywood Studios in Orlando.

Baseball, especially pitching, has always been one of my passions. In the spring of 2012, we had an away game just outside Raleigh. I was on tour with Brad Paisley at the time, but Brad took April off, which allowed me to make most of my games my senior year. *Johnny Johnson Photography*

I love golf and have played since I was pretty young. I've had the opportunity to play some great courses, including Pinehurst No. 2 and Pebble Beach. Here, I'm chipping in a ball on Number 12, a part of "Amen Corner" at Augusta National in Georgia.

Congratulating *American Idol*'s Season 11 winner Phillip Phillips after the May 2012 finale in Los Angeles—a really nice guy who had a huge hit titled "Home." A few hours earlier, I had the honor of presenting him with his trophy.

My friend Stephanie Shaffer was the director of White Deer Park in Garner in 2012. Stephanie handmade this sign using old license plates. Pretty much sums me up.

I love a great beach. Performing on the ocean is as good as it gets. Here, I'm singing at the Patriotic Festival in Virginia Beach. Since it wasn't too far from Garner, I drove there. When I got close, I passed some girls with their windows down, jamming to my music. I yelled out, "Hope you like it!" They freaked. It was pretty cool.

Accepting the *USA Today* Breakthrough Video Award
at the CMT Awards show in June 2012. The Band
Perry was on hand to present me with the award.
At the time, I was with Reid, Kimberly, and
Neil Perry on Brad Paisley's Virtual Reality Tour.

My first major tour was opening for Brad Paisley. What a great guy, surrounded by a great team! Brad invited me to join him each night onstage. This photo is from our last night of the Virtual Reality Tour at the Hollywood Bowl in October 2012.

On the set of a Bojangles' commercial in one of their restaurants in Raleigh, North Carolina. I had my band appear with me in three of the commercials, and we had a great time.

The Grand Ole Opry is one of my favorite places to perform. I love to cover country classics here, including Conway Twitty's "Hello Darlin'" and George Jones's "The Grand Tour." *Sara Kauss/ Getty Images*

At a show during the 2012 Paisley tour, this little boy caught my mom's eye. My fans come in all sizes and ages.

Attending his very first concert as he approached ninety years of age is Mr. Robert Hollowell of Hertford, North Carolina. His family attended my 2013 Labor Day Weekend show at Roanoke Festival Park in Manteo, North Carolina.

The "State Eight," along with some dads, attending an NC State basketball game in Ohio in 2013. One of my favorite things to do is pack my red tour bus, "The Wolfpack Express," with friends and catch a great sporting event.

Onstage with Mr. and Mrs. Wuf and NC State's spirited cheerleaders at our school's opening event called Packapolooza—August 2014, Hillsborough Street, Raleigh. *NC State University*

Packapolooza at NC State in Raleigh.
Eric Adkins © 2014

The legendary Charlie Wilson invited me to sing with him when he performed in Raleigh in February 2015. What a great guy! I discovered his music in my early teens.
P Music Group/ Elpwe Ray

My dad and I had the once-in-a-lifetime opportunity to see our Patriots win Super Bowl XLIX in February 2015 in Arizona. I was asked to sing for the Patriots pre–Super Bowl management party. One of the perks was getting tickets to the big game. The one downer was Dad got caught speeding on a traffic cam in Maricopa County, Arizona. The ticket was waiting for him when we got home.

I was honored to finally meet Jamey Johnson, songwriter and singer of the huge hit "In Color." We were both performing this night at the historic Ryman Auditorium in Nashville in January 2015.
Beverly Keel

Scotty McCreery, meet Scotty McCreery. The day I performed at the Illinois State Fair in 2015, a steer named after me was selected as the Grand Champion. Here, I'm pictured with its owner, Taylor Donelson, and Illinois governor Bruce Rauner.
Steve Smedley,
The Pantagraph

I surprise the chorus at my former elementary school just before they begin to sing my first single, "I Love You This Big." *Raleigh News & Observer*

Jim Carson, or just "Carson." Our lovable and ever-present merch guy, who has worked for some of the biggest names in the industry for more than thirty years. Look for him at our shows. *Douglas Field*

2015 Fall Fashion photo shoot for
Nash Country Weekly.
Jeremy Ryan

PART 2

LIFE AFTER *AMERICAN IDOL*

The Journey Continues

Chapter Seven

My Motley Crew

The first guy I interview to be my tour manager has only been around us a few minutes before I'm suspicious he's lying.

"I grew up in Raleigh, but I was born in this little town nobody's ever heard of," he says. "Elizabeth City."

I look over toward my mom. It's obvious he's done his homework on our family, but I think he's swinging a bit too far for the fences. Since being thrown in a business she knows little about, she's taken the approach of "trust, but verify." Things are no different for this potential tour manager. So she begins to grill the man with one question after another about Elizabeth City and about his family.

"Really? So what hospital were you born in?"

"Albemarle Hospital," he says.

"What county is it?" Mom asks.

She keeps asking questions. Soon it becomes apparent the man is telling the truth. In fact, we realize he and my mom were born in the same hospital only five months apart.

Our connection with Mike Childers is instantaneous. We will learn later that my late granddad,

R. P. Cooke, a North Carolina state trooper, gave Mike's uncle his first speeding ticket. When the judge suspended his uncle's driver's license for more than a year, my granddad went to the judge and asked him to reinstate his license so Mike's uncle could work and drive to school. Sounds hokey, but my granddad was a real-life Andy Griffith. Mike's family still attends the same church in Elizabeth City that my grandmother attends.

Oh, and one other interesting connection we would find out. That day in Milwaukee while we were in the stands listening to Danny Gokey greet us? Danny's tour manager was right behind him on the floor. So when Danny gave his memorable declaration that "the next American Idol is going to come from these auditions in my hometown—Milwaukee, Wisconsin!"—his tour manager rolled his eyes and chuckled.

Yeah, right.

His tour manager's name? Mike Childers.

He'd be the first guy I'd officially hire.

DIVINE INTERVENTION

Meeting Mike is one of the many providential moments during my musical journey when I saw God's hand on my life. I'm blessed to have been surrounded by the right people at exactly the right time. As the Idols *LIVE!* Tour drew to a close and my album release approached, I knew I needed to hire a tour manager. I was going to hit the ground running and needed someone who could run faster than I could.

Little did I know that this man would be waiting for God to open a door. Waiting and fasting after leaving his job. He'd been playing drums and working as a tour manager for Danny Gokey, but Mike got to a point where he put down the drumsticks and told his wife he didn't want to play anymore.

"Let's fast about it," she told him.

Mike, a man known for his sweet tooth and love of anything salty or fried, didn't exactly leap at his wife's suggestion. Yet he knew it was the right thing to do. So his fast lasted until he received a perfectly timed phone call.

"Hey, Mike," a manager he knew said. "I know you're from North Carolina, and my client's from North Carolina. So I'm wondering—have you ever thought about not drumming and just being a tour manager?"

He told her an emphatic yes. She explained to Mike that they had two *American Idol* finalists working for them. He stopped her right there before she continued.

"I really don't want to tour manage a teenage girl," Mike said. "I have one of those right now."

"We have the girl covered. I want you to meet Scotty."

All Mike had ever known was drumming, some-times tour managing at the same time, but he knew it was a God thing. Travel arrangements were made right away for him to meet me on the road. While at the airport, Mike decided to end his fast by finding a celebratory Cinnabon.

On the afternoon he shows up to meet me, I'm trying to live up to my MIA nickname. We're in Philadelphia, and the Phillies ar playing that evening, so I'm planning to watch my five innings. I get a call around 3:00 p.m. from my manager at the time, Ann Edelblute. She tells me about a guy named Mike coming over to be interviewed for a tour manager position.

"Are you kiddin' me?" I tell her. "I got a game I'm trying to go to."

Ann happens to be Carrie Underwood's manager as well, so she knows Mike, who played drums for Carrie at one time. Mike's brother is also Carrie's bandleader. I know that if Ann set this up, she really feels this will be a good fit.

By the time I meet Mike, I'm inwardly sulking at the fact that I can't go see a few innings of baseball. I know, I know. It's not the most impressive way to meet someone you'll be spending the next half of the decade with.

Once I spend some time with Mike and realize he *isn't* lying about all the connections we have with him, it's a no-brainer. I *have* to hire him. He's smart, good-natured, and funny and has been in the business long enough to know what to do and what not to do. He's got a head full of black hair. It's amazing how quickly I turn it gray.

The next day, Mike officially begins working. And he has no time to celebrate or allow for downtime.

It's August 17. My album is scheduled to release on October 4.

SCRAMBLIN' MAN

Hurricane Irene destroys my first band. This would be a tragic thing, except—well, I never actually have a chance to meet them.

From the moment I hire Mike, he begins working on putting together everything for me. Since I was a part of the *Idol* machine, the solo artist Scotty McCreery is basically starting from scratch. I need lots of things. A band, a crew, credentials, a rider, stage plans, facial hair—*everything.*

Mike ends up enlisting his brother, Mark, to help hire the guys in the band. So by September, we have a band ready and rehearsing the songs I'll be doing for the upcoming events planned for the album release. That includes doing performances on *Ellen* and *The Tonight Show with Jay Leno.* Coming off the biggest show in the world, I thought nothing of it. Just figured it was normal. My band, however, was amazed, shocked, flabbergasted. They were about to do all these shows in one week—with a seventeen-year-old! They've worked their whole lives for this kind of thing.

Then the hurricane hits. Those first few gigs get canceled since they're in the New York area. For a variety of reasons, four of the guys in the band who have been rehearsing decide to bail. I can only imagine what their reasons are.

Who knows. The only one who decides to stay is Joey Sanchez, our current drummer.

While Joey may be my longest-tenured band member, all the guys in the band are my favorites because each of them brings a unique element to our group. The way things turned out, I really do believe God wanted me with *this* set of guys. I'm not saying He made a hurricane in order for that to happen. But as the saying goes, the Lord works in mysterious ways. Right?

Yet before the rest of the crew is found, my band only consists of a drummer.

Needless to say, Mike is scrambling. He calls his brother to talk about hiring a guitarist they worked with when they both played for Danny Gokey. Matt Reviere joins our team as the bandleader. Matt ends up calling two guys he knows and trusts—Justin Ward and Jeff Harper. After our first bassist spent only a short time with us, Nathan Thomas joins us. I still consider him to be one of the originals.

They all arrive at the scene after finding themselves at a crossroad in their lives.

Matt Reviere was actually fasting with his wife as he considered another job when he got the call. Just like Mike. He was waiting on God to show him what he should be doing next in his career.

Jeff, who would end up being a guitarist, backup singer, and keyboardist, had just finished a gig with Love and Theft and didn't know where he'd be next. Matt knew Jeff was great and told him he needed to join us. Matt and Jeff were best friends, so it seemed to be a perfect decision.

Our honorary Canadian and steel guitar player, Justin, had worked with Mike Childers before. The joke is that Justin hadn't actually *spoken* to Mike in the year or so they were together. Justin can be a quiet guy. Until you get to know him. Lord help you if you do!

After the first bassist departed, Matt auditioned several guys for the job. When Nathan arrived for the audition, he quickly assumed he wasn't going to get it. The other three guys who auditioned were all friends of Matt. Nathan knew he didn't stand a chance.

After having played in the Christian music industry for a decade, Nathan was burned out. Joey was the one who had given Nathan's number to Matt. Like all the other guys, Nathan seemed to fit. He was someone who understood what faith meant, but he didn't wear it on his T-shirt like some kind of trendy slogan. After playing for Matt, however, Nathan left feeling like he'd blown it, knowing he could have given a better performance.

Nathan says that when Matt called him afterward, he answered with the best Eeyore impression he could give. He really believed he hadn't gotten the job.

"Wow," Matt told him. "So do you want this or not?"

That shows the character of Matt—and really of the whole band. Guys who want the best.

Nathan has said that in some ways, all the guys had been at points in their lives where they finally prayed to God, saying they wanted and needed a change. They admitted it and then asked for a door to open.

The funny—and ironic—part about this is that none of them really knew the guy standing at the door.

Here are some initial responses after hearing the name Scotty McCreery.

"What's his name again?"

"Country has never been my thing."

"I've never watched *American Idol*."

"I'll have to go on YouTube and check him out."

Even Mike had only heard of me in an offhanded way when his relatives in Elizabeth City told him to check out this sweet young man from North Carolina singing country music on *Idol*.

I think it's pretty cool how the guys end up coming to play for me. And they don't have weeks to make the decision. In just a matter of days, we'll be going on national television in front of millions. They have music to learn. Fast.

MOTLEY CREW

I've sung in front of Jennifer Lopez, Steven Tyler, Beyoncé, and Lady Gaga. I've done duets with Josh Turner and Tim McGraw. I've been in front of thousands and have had millions watching me from their homes. Yet when I first meet this eclectic band of brothers I'll play with for the next five years, I'm scared to death.

I'd heard of guys like this in Nashville for a while now—professional musicians who take their jobs seriously and are very good at what they do. This wasn't LA anymore. I was genuinely nervous to meet and perform with them. I can play the part of being cool and laid-back, but they could tell right away I was anxious.

These guys have had a little time to learn more about me, so they're coming with their own set of nerves and expectations. Things like suddenly picking up a *USA Today* and seeing my face on the front page or looking at YouTube videos of performances have made them realize what's happened in my life. They're also aware of how the first single and album have blown up.

Joey is the most talkative of the bunch. We will end up laughing at how we eventually introduce him in shows as "the Italian Stallion," even though his last name is Sanchez. He's a kooky nut! He's from Seattle, loves Pearl Jam, and has a nice sarcastic wit about him. *Nice? Did I just say nice?* He demonstrates it that first day of auditions after watching me with my phone.

"Do you know you're the first person in history who's going to have a number one record while carrying a busted phone?"

I chuckle and look down at the cracked screen on my iPhone. I'd actually gotten used to it.

Jeff is a jolly young guy who just appreciates being here. He smiles a lot. I mean—watch him in concert even now. He'll be wearing a big ole grin and some ripped jeans. He knows a lot about music and has this good nature about him that's impossible not to like.

On the first day of rehearsal with Scotty and his band, we realized Scotty had a nervous tick: practicing a golf swing. He must have gone through thirty-six holes at Augusta National before the first rehearsal was over.

MIKE CHILDERS, TOUR MANAGER

Justin might be reserved, but he can play anything. He's also got a great sense of humor, but he shows it in the Canadian way—the casual and agreeable manner.

They've all heard the music but haven't ever heard the lyrics to the songs. We have three days.

THE TROUBLE WITH PITCHES

I'm watching *The Tonight Show with Jay Leno* and sweating. We taped the performance earlier that day, and everything went great, except . . . Except for that one note.

It wasn't so good.

Yeah, it was pretty bad actually.

All of us are on the bus watching the screen and waiting. Before leaving the set, Mike told me he'd have a conversation with the sound tech for the show. There are things you can do to help adjust bad mistakes like that. The crazy thing is that I've been doing this for how many months now, but on *live* television.

Maybe the whole taped thing messed me up.

The moment is approaching. Mike gives me a look. We all seem to hold our breaths. The chord comes, and it sounds fine. I breathe a sigh of relief. Mike shouts out a "yes," as if Alabama just scored a touchdown, thanking the sound guy by name.

Singing off-key is really, thankfully, a rarity for me. A lot of people compliment my voice by saying it sounds live just like it does on my records. Some singers need a little or even a lot of assistance in the studio, but my voice has always been consistent without a ton of auto-tune. I'm thankful for that.

Every now and then, however, you let one get away from you.

It's like pitching. Sometimes you throw a wild one and end up hitting the batter.

Thankfully, for this big introduction to so many in the country, I get to change the trajectory of that wild pitch. Just don't tell anybody I told you.

TALK SHOWS

One of the most fun things my band and I get to do is perform on talk shows and news shows. They can be a bit stressful. Sometimes they're live, not taped. There's *The View* I mentioned earlier—my very first TV appearance, even earlier than *Idol*, thanks to Nigel Lythgoe. Until then, I never paid much attention to talk shows. High school guys are doing lots of things, and watching talk shows usually isn't one of them. *The View* gave me my very first lesson that talk shows have a huge following. They can make your phone blow up instantaneously.

Appearing on *Ellen* was a blast. She made me breathe helium from a balloon and then talk. The result was, you guessed it, pretty dang funny. Then there's the time Conan O'Brien mispronounced my name, which resulted in a hysterical fan correction skit you can find on YouTube.

The first time I appeared on *Leno*, one of his guests beat him up for wearing denim on denim. I was in the green room watching this exchange. Guess what I had brought along to wear? Denim on denim—you know, jeans with a denim shirt. Man, I dreaded walking onto that stage.

The coolest thing about talk shows and news shows are the talented people you meet. I've had the honor of working with journalists such as Lester Holt on NBC, Robin Roberts on ABC, Elisabeth Hasselbeck and Steve Doocy on Fox, and CNN and HLN journalists such as Rebecca Baer, Ashley Vaughan, Christi Paul, and Natasha Curry.

You also meet incredible celebrities on these talk shows. Tim Allen was on *Leno* one night when I performed. I thought, *Man, I'm talking to Buzz Lightyear and Santa Claus!* I also bumped into Theresa Caputo, the "Long Island Medium," while on the set of *Leno*. We ran into each other in the hallway. She told me she and her daughter, Victoria, were big fans and then pointed to the sky.

"They're telling me you're so grounded."

Hmmm, I thought.

She went on to tell me how my late granddad watches me all the time.

Now that was pretty cool to hear.

ANOTHER HOMECOMING

Five days after the release of my debut album, *Clear as Day*, I'm turning eighteen. And just like the title of my album, it's obvious how I should celebrate. Some artists might head to Vegas or the Bahamas to celebrate with friends, but I know there's only one place I want to be.

Home.

So we plan on having a special "album release" homecoming concert in Raleigh. The concert will be October 8, one day before I turn eighteen on October 9. People can even get in free if they have my new CD with them or purchase one at the gate. FYE Records is there to assist. We pick Time Warner Cable Music Pavilion at Walnut Creek, since it's a sensible place for a music event like this. An added bonus: Garner is just five minutes away from Walnut Creek.

When I tell the band we'll be playing here for the album release, I can tell they're not exactly impressed.

A free show for friends and family? Starting around lunchtime?

They will tell me later they're expecting maybe

a couple hundred people or so. Around fifteen thousand fans show up for the show. My bandmates are surprised—something they'll continue to be for a while until what exactly has happened to my world sinks in.

The incredible thing here isn't me; it's what's happened to me and what kind of a crazy ride we're all on.

Marty Young and Janie Carothers from WQDR introduce me to the lively and loud crowd.

"It's been a bit of whirlwind for you, huh?" Janie says.

"It's been insane," I say. "This last week we've been in Nashville, New York, LA, and now Raleigh, North Carolina."

The screams from the crowd actually drown out the next thing I say.

"I think everybody's glad you're back," Janie says.

Once again, I'm able to thank everyone for their support during my *Idol* run and also for the incredible hometown visit.

The inevitable questions come up. About singing and songs and music and—

"You're single, right?" Janie asks.

Hey now.

Screams.

This is crazy.

"What do you look for in a girl?" Marty asks.

"I'm looking for a nice down-home hometown

girl," I end up saying. "I'm not looking for a Hollywood Barbie doll. Nothing like that."

I share what my future looks like—about heading to school, tours, music hopes. The cool thing is I grew up coming to this venue and watching musicians play. Soon I'm doing the thing I'm most comfortable doing. I sing half a dozen songs and have thousands of my friends singing along with me. There's only one song I don't sing with them.

"Happy birthday, dear Scotty! Happy birthday to you!"

And as if that's not enough for a birthday celebration, afterward I get to sing the national anthem before the NC State football game against Central Michigan.

The Wolfpack doesn't let me down. They give me a nice present—a 38–24 victory.

EIGHTEEN

I'm eighteen years old. I can finally vote.

For a moment, I'm able to stop and try to find some perspective. The reality, however, is that it's impossible to fully make sense of everything.

There's been this thing I've always known— this thing, deep down, I've always believed. It's that somehow and someway I'd end up doing some-thing with my music. Something. But I never saw all of this coming, especially so soon.

I've been singing all my life, and now I'm being asked to do this all the time. I'm being paid to do it. I'm being applauded and pushed along by all these people. As I told the folks at the concert in Raleigh, it's incredible that I get paid to sing. It's my life's love, and I don't think I'll ever look at it as a job.

God has always blessed me with support, but now it's truly surrounding me. Time and time again, I'm brought back down to earth by seeing all these people investing their time and money and *love* in me.

In ordinary Scotty McCreery?

Where do You want me to go? This is what I ask God.

I know the plans I have for you. This is what I hear Him tell me.

He's not going to reveal all those plans right now. That's what this trust thing is all about. But so far, He's been very, very gracious. I just need to honor those blessings and the blessings of others by staying on this path and doing the right things. With my music and my education, but most of all with my life.

Chapter Eight

Girls, Goals, Garner . . . and Brad

I've been looking for the text for thirty minutes, and I still can't find it. I swear it was sent the night I won *Idol*, but then again, *a lot* of texts were sent that night.

It's late September 2011, and I'm back home for Garner's homecoming game. I'm trying to find a message from Gabi Dugal, but I'm having to look at each message since I don't have her name in my phone. I'm starting to wonder if I'm remembering right, until I find the short and sweet text.

Hey, Scotty! Big congrats on winning tonight!

I can see I never replied to it.
Well, I'm only four months late.
I'm still irritated that Gabi didn't win "homecoming queen" tonight. She was on the field with a perfect dress and looked beautiful. She was robbed. Something in me just has to tell her this.

It's bogus you didn't win tonight. If it'd been my choice, you'd have won.

Cheesy, I know.

I'm not sure if she's going to reply. Maybe it'll take her four months. But thankfully I get a message right back. We start talking that night—well, texting, which is the next best thing. I'm able to tell her how great she looked. We joked around and spent a long time going back and forth.

We've talked every day since then.

It's funny 'cause Gabi and I have known each other almost all our lives. She doesn't believe me when I say I liked her in kindergarten. But we have proof she liked me. In a diary she kept then, she has "Mrs. Gabi McCreery" written all over it, with little hearts drawn next to it.

And thanks to *Idol*, there is music, and later there are music videos. And one of those videos happened to need a leading lady.

THE TROUBLE WITH WIGGINS

So the label decides that "The Trouble with Girls" is going to be the next single off *Clear as Day*. It's a fun song that really represents the guy I happen to be. A senior in high school who's never really dated a lot and who doesn't quite understand females. Since we were going to shoot the video at a high school, I suggested the obvious.

"Why don't we go to Garner and shoot with my friends and the people I've known my whole life?"

So that's exactly what Director Roman White

decides to do. It's a blast. We spend half of a Saturday filming the video around school, going from the hallways to a science room to the cafeteria and finally to the baseball field. If anybody is ever curious about what Garner Magnet High looked like, I just tell them to watch that video.

Gabi plays a key role in the video, and it comes because of a suggestion I make to the director. The video starts with me walking down the hallway with a buddy of mine, Kyle Wiggins. I think about this and find it a bit odd.

"Hey, Roman," I say. "Don't you think it's weird in a song called 'The Trouble with Girls' that I'm walking down the hallway with a *guy?*"

"No, I think it's cool," he says.

"I think it's weird," I tell him.

I motion to the students who are here to help us out today.

"See that girl over there in the purple?" I ask.

"Yeah."

"Why don't I walk with her?"

Now, in case you're wondering—no, that outline of someone with broad shoulders wearing shorts who is walking next to me at the start of the video is *not* Gabi. Yes, it's Wiggins. But the director does end up using her for the starring role.

It's just one more cool way of my regular life intersecting with my musical one. It's also a nice way to keep Gabi and me talking.

SHORT-TERM AND LONG-TERM

My senior year is a case of living in-between—doing life as a senior in high school and doing life as a new country musician, suddenly touring and doing promotion for his record-breaking album. I know some industry folks aren't thrilled at the idea of me being at school. They want me to totally focus on my career and all the buzz happening around it. I'm still working hard at my music. But I know I'm only eighteen once. I will only have a senior year of high school with these friends I've grown up with *one time*. If I skip this, I won't get it back.

My AP English teacher, Mrs. Still, asks us to work on a booklet we'll finish by the end of the year called "My Philosophy of Life." I still have the book, and it's interesting to read through the entries. The first entry is about goals. It's fun to read now, since it's hard to remember that guy.

Goals

How do you go from where you are to where you wanna be? And I think you have to have an enthusiasm for life.
You have to have a dream, a goal.
And you have to be willing to work for it.

JIM VALVANO

In my eyes, goals are by far one of the most important aspects of a person's life. They give us purpose and a direction. Without goals, why do we get out of bed in the morning? Larry Bird once said, "A winner is somebody who recognizes his God-given talents, works his tail off to develop them into skills, and uses these skills to accomplish his goals." Bird wanted to be the best basketball player who ever lived. This was a long-term goal for him. In another conversation, Bird said he wanted to "first master the fundamentals." This would have been a short-term goal for him. We all have both. You could make the analogy to a ladder. Each rung up the ladder is one of our short-term goals, leading us higher and higher until we ultimately reach our long-term goal.

A recent short-term goal of mine has been to come back to school, work hard, and walk at graduation with my class. Many people questioned my ability to return to school after winning *American Idol*. I had to keep telling them time and time again that it is just what I wanted to do. I was determined to come back, fit in among my peers, make good grades, play baseball, and do all the things a normal high school senior would do—all while staying current with my music career. It has not been easy, but so far I believe things are working out quite well. Pretty soon, I will be moving on to college. That will be a whole new animal to tackle, but I cannot wait for the challenge.

Many of my short-term goals will be like stepping-stones, guiding me along the way to goals I ultimately want to accomplish. In ten years, I will be twenty-eight. A lot will have changed by then. At twenty-eight years of age, I see myself as a family man, with a great wife and maybe even a child. This may be a little soon, but a lot can happen in ten years. I also see myself as a successful country music singer. It is too soon to tell whether my career will last five years or thirty years, but I do know I have goals. In ten years, I want to be at the top of the charts. I want to have at least five albums under my belt, and I would like to be headlining my own tour and selling out major venues. These are all things that will take work, but I am willing to put forth the time and effort to make these things happen.

All in all, goals are ideas we would like to accomplish over time through hard work and dedication. The legacy I want to leave behind, however, is not necessarily based on all my accomplishments; I want people to remember me by the hard work I put in to make those things happen. I want them to remember the person, the artist, the husband, and the father I was, never wavering from my core values and beliefs through everything that happened to me.

Four years after writing that essay, I still feel the same way. I know more about the music industry and have succeeded in some ways and have a long way to go in others. No little Johnny and June McCreery twins running around the house.

All in due time and in God's will.

But the dreams are still there, just like they were in my senior year of high school.

O SAY CAN YOU HEAR?

Dreams are great. But now and then, unfortunately, you end up having nightmares.

I'm at Game One of the World Series between the St. Louis Cardinals and Texas Rangers at Busch Stadium in St. Louis. It's October 19, 2011, and I'm getting ready to sing the national anthem in front of millions. It's exciting, and I'm pumped and ready to sing.

Right before I sing, Lance Corporal James Sperry of the Marines is introduced, along with his five-year-old daughter. He served and was wounded in Iraq. He's being honored for the rescue-and-recovery efforts in Joplin, Missouri, hours after the tornado hit there. Alongside Sperry and his daughter are the wives of the president and vice president—Michelle Obama and Jill Biden.

As they're being introduced, I'm handed a microphone. It only takes a few seconds before realizing the awful truth. I look over at my tour manager, Mike.

"It's not on," I tell him. I'm not able to turn this on myself. It has to be turned on remotely.

Earlier in the day, we did a sound check to prevent this very thing from happening. They had actually purchased an in-ear system after our team made the request, since we know that the delay in a stadium can be pretty brutal. The sound check left us feeling confident, since it goes off without a hitch.

Mike rushes over to the producer standing closest to us and shares the situation. After contacting the sound engineer upstairs, the producer doesn't seem to be worried.

"It'll be on when it needs to be on," he tells us.

I see Mike giving me a not-so-comforting look of complete doubt. I wonder if I'm giving him the same.

The announcer's voice suddenly thunders above our heads.

"Ladies and gentlemen, please rise and remove your caps for our national anthem."

With dozens of military men holding a massive American flag right in front of me, I'm introduced to the thousands in the stadium.

"Performing tonight's anthem is 2011 *American Idol* winner with the number one country album—Scotty McCreery!"

The crowd gives a brief round of welcome applause and then quickly becomes quiet in order to hear my rendition of this honorable song. I hold up my microphone and begin to sing.

This is what it sounds like for the people in the stadium, along with folks watching at home.

Crickets.

All you can hear are the faint echoes of the crowd talking, the flag flapping, and the wind whipping around the ballpark. I don't realize at first that no one can hear me.

And now for the sweet, silent sounds of Scotty McCreery!

Yep—the mic is *still* off.

Albert Pujols, the Cardinals first baseman, turns toward me. We make eye contact, and he says,

"No mic." The same producer grabs a wired microphone nearby and gives it to me. I get to start over.

How many people are watching this again?

I don't even think about it. I just focus on the song and sing it with all I've got. No technical difficulties are going to bring me down.

As for any haters out there—well, I'm doubting they'll ever reach this point in the book to criticize my description of how well I perform. But I quickly learn that singing the national anthem makes you a surefire target on a slow news day. Some ridiculous writer comes up with a story saying I sang "No Jose" instead of "O say." Seriously? Yes, I'm a quarter Hispanic, and someone honestly thinks I'd sing that? Even my label has to get involved and make a statement.

Lesson learned—several of them, in fact.

THE TROUBLE WITH LIP-SYNCHING

It's a few days before Thanksgiving 2011. I'm packing my bags to head to New York to appear in the Macy's Thanksgiving Day Parade. I find myself thinking back to a year ago. I was doing the same thing, getting my suitcase ready to go to Hollywood Week.

It really does seem like yesterday. The months didn't just fly by. It's like I skipped them all together and then was given a flash drive of all the memories.

The *Idol* experience had so many—too many—blessings to be thankful for. Moments like being mentored by someone like Jimmy Iovine and meeting Muhammad Ali at his awesome fight night event. But since winning, the list has grown, beginning with winning the proceeds to make my first album. But I also win lots of other things. One of those is a chance to perform at Disney and ride in the Disney parade. Later I sing for their holiday parade, which airs on Christmas Day. This gives me a chance to start a relationship with a fabulous organization.

Come on . . . who *doesn't* love Disney?

From 2009 to 2014, an exhibit called "The *American Idol* Experience" is open at Disney's Hollywood Studios. It's fun because it emulates what we went through on *Idol* by giving park guests a chance to audition in front of live audiences that vote on the winner. Over the years, I'm invited to surprise audiences by coming onstage and saying hello.

Okay, I'll be honest. I kept coming back for those "Fast Pass" tickets. I'm a sucker for some of those rides. I did love surprising the guests, but I love those fast Disney rides just as much.

A couple of weeks ago, I performed "Walk in the Country" at the Country Music Association Awards and had the opportunity to announce the

"Radio Stations of the Year" award. Now I'm heading out to an appearance on the *Today* show to celebrate my new album being certified gold, as well as to sing my new single.

The day after performing on *Today*, I'm standing in the Macy's Thanksgiving Day Parade on a giant muffin pan surrounded by life-sized cupcakes and lots of bakers. I'm riding high on the Morton Salt Home Baked Goodness float.

I've been on the float for a while, waving at people as my music plays. I'm holding a microphone, but it's quite obvious I'm not singing. For a while, I just say hi and don't even try to pretend. But as we slow down and prepare for my performance on live television, I know I have to go through the motions of singing. I've never lip-synched before, but how hard can it be? Right?

Scotty McCreery begins singing "The Trouble with Girls" while I stand there holding my mic down at my chest.

Oh yeah, bring it to your mouth. Duh!

The previous night, at the parade sound check, there are no fans, no screams. But the day of the live parade, you can't hear the start of the song because of the screams.

I don't act like anything unusual just happened, and I sing the whole song. It's a simple and honest mistake. I'm sure there'll be lots more to come.

The Internet sure has a field day with this one.

"Lip-synch fail"

"Lip-synch disaster"

"Lip-synch oops!"

I later see a news report from someone who says she's a huge *Idol* fan. I guess the reporter never heard them call me "Scotty," as she introduces me as Scott McCreery.

"He had a massive lip-synch flub at the Thanksgiving parade, and I was horrified because he's a good singer . . ."

Let's see here.

"Massive."

"Flub."

"Horrified."

Here's the truth, and you need to brace yourselves . . .

Everybody lip-synchs at the Macy's Thanksgiving Day Parade. They don't give you an option—you just do it. And here's some advice for you aspiring singers out there: Keep the microphone covering your lips *before* your song starts. I should have known that much, right? I mean, hey—I've been singing professionally for how long now? Six, seven months? Anyway, another lesson learned again—in front of millions. Sometimes you just got to remember the famous Teddy Roosevelt quote: "The only man who never makes a mistake is the man who never does anything."

That same night, the wonderful folks at Macy's fly me and my band to Atlanta to sing at the Macy's tree lighting event at the Lenox Square Mall. Except for the lip-synching hiccup, the day is incredible from start to finish. After being a part of these Macy's festivities, I had a new appreciation for the time and energy they invest in the holidays. They really do work to make the holidays brighter all over the country.

DATING

So one moment I'm flubbing with lip-synching, and the next I'm flubbing with the ladies.

One night while Gabi and I are hanging out with our friends, someone laughs and says something about the two of us dating. It's just a passing comment that neither of us respond to. The next day, however, I text her about it.

It's funny how they were joking about us dating.

She texts me back with a question.

Are we dating?

I look at my phone and think about this

question. Is this a joke? Is she trying to be ironic here? Or is she really wondering this? I text her back.

Are we not?

Good question.

I'm really confused here.

Are you joking?

Are you?

Again, this must be a trick question.

The trouble with girls is they're always two steps ahead of us guys.

After a little more conversation, it's obvious that the trouble with boys is they're a bit clueless. Boys might assume things, but we also might get those things wrong. I assumed for a while we were dating, but I guess I never asked to make it "Facebook official."

So the following day, I meet Gabi in the student parking lot at the end of the school. I find her smiling that smile and batting those eyes and suddenly not being a character in a music video but being the one you write those songs about.

"So you want to make this official?" I ask.

"Sure."

FIRST SIXTY-MINUTE CONCERT

It's okay, Scotty. Breathe in. Breathe out. It's okay.
It's moments before the show, and I'm scared to death. It's January 2012, and we're performing at the Murphy USA National Manager Meeting and Expo onsite at Disney World. This is where the Murphy Oil Corporation invites its managers for a meeting and spectacular event. The fun part of this expo comes when the company decides to do their own version of *Idol* this year, so they thought they'd surprise their employees by bringing me down to perform.

The terror isn't about who I'm singing for; it's about how many songs I'm going to be singing.

Up until now, I've always just sung one song or a few songs here and there. Even on the Idols *LIVE!* Tour, the songs were divided among various singers. But now I'm the only singer. This isn't going to be a solo in church or a couple of songs on a TV show. I'm singing for more than an hour.

One full hour.

Denise Kirk of Brattle Entertainment hired me for this gig. She knows it's my first long set. She's even flown down from Boston to Orlando to see how this goes.

Soon I find myself onstage, sweating and forgetting lyrics and getting little things wrong. Making mistakes in where I'm supposed to go or even in remembering which song is next. I'm barely eighteen and in the middle of a crash course in full-on concert performance. The good thing is that the band is helping me out and the crowd is definitely enjoying the show. Some even stand on their chairs.

I've learned something by now: The smartest people surround themselves with a good team. And I have one heck of a team in Mike and the rest of the band.

Our production manager, Jayme Braun, is a sharp and talented guy who works with this great team as well. Mike and Jayme also hired Jorie, a kid who was working at a church. Jorie is one of the hardest-working guys I've ever seen. He never stops moving and doing things.

These are two more in the great bunch of guys who surround me. This is the first true concert we do. But it certainly won't be the last.

We're just getting warmed up.

BIG NEWS

In the summer of 2011 while on the Idols *LIVE!* Tour, my manager gives me a call with the news.

"Brad Paisley wants you to tour with him next year."

Just like that, I've gone from fan to opening act.

It's hard to like country music and *not* be a big fan of Brad. There's a reason he's been so successful, and I believe it starts with him being a generous and fun-loving guy. It also helps to be insanely gifted. I can only dream of being able to play the guitar like he does.

It's fun to keep the upcoming tour a secret until Brad comes in concert to Raleigh later that month. While playing at the Walnut Creek Amphitheatre, he invites me onstage and asks me in front of the audience if I'd like to tour with him. I tell him yes, and he replies it's a done deal.

The tour—the Virtual Reality Tour—will begin January 12, 2012, in Grand Rapids, Michigan. Along with Brad, The Band Perry will be hitting the road with us.

At the time, none of us know the tour will last all year long and will take us to more than forty different venues across North America.

The tour is going to be a great opportunity for me and the band. But it will also be an opportunity to be able to get to know a great artist in this business.

GREATNESS

While touring with Brad Paisley, I witness what makes the guy tick. If I had to sum it up in three words, they would be *great role model.*

Brad shows me that a man in his position can still have a family and solid values. He's a good guy who shares lots of thoughts and advice that I soak up. He has fun and is generous with his time and resources. He's such a great example. He brings his kids on the road with him. His father happens to travel with him also.

At one point, Brad said this tour should be called "the Mamas and the Papas." Not only is Brad's dad, Doug, on the road with us, but we also have my parents and Ashley. Then there are The Band Perry's parents, Steve and Marie. Being around this sort of family atmosphere makes things a lot easier.

It's a great thing to have role models I can actually talk to and become friends with. I'm always looking around and learning how to do this whole music thing right. I'll never be perfect, but at least I can be focused in the right direction.

Brad's team may never fully understand how their generosity influenced my career. Not only did Brad share nuggets of insight; so did his dad and his tour manager Brent Long. They continued to introduce me to different folks in the industry. I'm only eighteen at this time and still a senior in high school. With every event, my family and I are trying to learn as much as possible, as quickly as possible, about this industry. That's why being with Brad's camp this early in my career was priceless.

While on the Paisley tour, we have the opportunity to meet a really interesting guy. We're in Camden, New Jersey, just across the river from

Philly. Brad's set has ended, and it's load-out time. My family and I are sitting around the dressing room when we get a knock at the door. A guy with graying hair enters.

"You don't know me, but my name is Hubie Synn, and I want to share something God has laid on my heart."

Hubie knows quite a bit about guitar amps and was a backstage guest that night. It turns out he is a traveling minister, author, and CPA who is said to have a prophetic gift. Hubie shares that God has great plans for me and that I should keep the faith. He looks over at Ashley and tells her the same thing. He tells her it won't happen as quickly for her, but God is going to do a work in her life also.

Wow. When he finishes, there isn't a dry eye in my dressing room. In this tough business, it's exactly the sort of pep talk we all needed.

THE DICHOTOMY

One minute, I'm performing in front of a rowdy general admission crowd in Nashville at the CMT Music Awards. I've just been handed a trophy with a big belt buckle for winning the award for Breakthrough Video of the Year. The following morning, I'm back in North Carolina at my high school graduation, walking with my classmates and receiving my diploma from Garner Magnet

High. The former is quite an honor since it's voted on by fans, but the latter is also something I'm proud to be receiving.

That morning after waking up, I tweet the following:

Ive enjoyed these last 4 years. wouldnt trade any of them for the world. #iamatrojan

I'm glad to be *here* standing with all 462 of my classmates. The kids I grew up with. The ones who will forever still think of me as Scotty— the guy who went on that TV show and now is able to make country music.

I'm looking ahead to next year. NC State University awaits me. I'll be living with my guys in an apartment near campus. I'll also be continuing to tour and working on a new album.

I tell the media I'm not doing any interviews after our high school graduation ceremony. This morning and celebration are not about me but about the whole senior class.

Zach Wilson nails it at the opening of his valedictorian speech: "First and foremost, above all, I have to give thanks to Jesus Christ because without Him I would be nothing."

Garner Magnet High is not a private Christian school. That's just the kind of school I've grown up with and the sort of people I've been around.

Zach decides to forgo the cheesy memories and

typical inspirational rhetoric. He gives his address by quoting song titles and lyrics only.

"At Garner, I've had the time of my life," Zach says. "Sure we had those days when we were under pressure, living on a prayer, saying we don't need no education. But we've been taking care of business through all those times."

I don't know how many songs he refers to, but it's gotta number almost a hundred. It's a brilliant speech that's funny, moving, and perfect. And hey—it even mentions one of my songs.

So live like you're dying—that's certainly the next thing on my list. Soon you'll walk this way and this will be another day in the life. But don't worry. Be happy now. That's my prerogative.

Someday when our lives have passed us by, I'll lay around and wonder why you guys were always there for me. Because there'll always be something there to remind me of my water tower town, Garner. And don't you forget about me and I hope you don't become someone I used to know. Call me maybe. Thanks for the memories. Take care and let the good times roll.

Well said, Zach. Well said.

It's a perfect way to say good-bye to Garner and to welcome the days ahead.

Chapter Nine

The Greatest Gift

It's December 2013.

I'm at the tree-lighting ceremony at Rockefeller Center in New York City, yuckin' it up with an older guy who's one of the funniest people I've ever been around. He's behind the stage with me, and we're talking about the "Holly Jolly" Christmas song I just sang, as well as about the cold and the crowd. I don't think anything of it until my mom asks me if I knew who I was talking to. I just shake my head.

"That's Billy Crystal!" she informs me.

"Really?"

Moments later, NBC's Savannah Guthrie confirms it when she says she's joined by the "legendary" Billy Crystal and Bette Midler on stage.

I guess you've been to a lot of celebrity events when you stop looking for those very people. Both Billy and I are here to promote our latest ventures—his family film called *Parental Guidance* and my Christmas album, *Christmas with Scotty McCreery*.

Some may think having a holiday album out only a year after my first release is too quick, but it really turns out to be a great decision, for both professional and personal reasons.

ECHOES OF THE PAST

Let's back up four months. It's July 2013, and I'm in the recording studio trying to picture chestnuts roasting on an open fire. Well, I've never actually been around chestnuts roasting anywhere. But we're recording a Christmas album in the middle of summer, so we're all trying to get into the spirit. We have a Christmas tree in the studio, along with Christmas lights decorating the music stand. Every now and then, I put on one of the Santa hats we brought. We even had Christmas cookies and cupcakes delivered when we began recording.

Sure, it's almost a hundred degrees outside, but I can still sing, "Let it snow, let it snow, let it snow."

The idea for doing a Christmas album came from a variety of holiday-inspired events I did last year. Yes, there was the Macy's Thanksgiving Day Parade and the Macy's Atlanta tree lighting, but there was also the Raleigh Christmas Parade, for which I happened to serve as grand marshal. That same season, I performed "The First Noel" on a Christmas special for ABC called *CMA Country Christmas*. Disney also asked me to sing for their Christmas Day special. There's nothing like the festive feel of sweat rolling down your neck while wearing your coat and scarf on an eighty-degree day in front of Cinderella's castle.

All of these things planted seeds.

With school and touring, the thought of getting another album of new music released in 2012 is impossible. We all realize two years will pass without a new album out there. You don't want the world to forget about you, of course. And you want to make sure you continue to give your fans new music.

Because the holidays are so special, it feels like a natural fit to move forward with a Christmas album. My label gives the thumbs-up for the project. And what a great move. Not only did it bring about a bunch of great opportunities, like the tree-lighting ceremony, but *Christmas with Scotty* is certified gold, with sales of half a million units just three weeks after its release.

After the project was approved, I immediately cleared a week in my schedule the next month to get into the studio ASAP. Instead of having to find nuggets of time and random recording studios like I did for *Clear as Day*, I'm able to work in a more casual manner in the same studio for the entire album. Mark Bright is once again the producer. The process ends up feeling like a bunch of friends getting together to sing Christmas carols.

I get to put a Scotty McCreery spin on songs like

"Winter Wonderland," "Jingle Bells," and "Holly Jolly Christmas." My favorite Elvis Christmas song, "Santa Claus Is Back in Town," is included on the album. I even record two original songs.

Here's a fun fact about "Santa Claus Is Back in Town." Paul Leim, the drummer, had actually been playing drums for "Elvis: The Concert," a late nineties tour that featured Elvis's voice with live musicians. While at Starstruck recording Elvis's Christmas tune, Paul lets loose with a little "C.C. Rider" at the end of the song. This is a classic cover Elvis loved to do. I jump in and hang tight with my best "C.C. Rider." The studio's suddenly on fire, and the musicians are going crazy. It's not rehearsed, and we do just one take.

It makes us wonder—should it make the album? Both Mark Bright and Brian Wright, my A&R guy at the label, say absolutely. You gotta hear it on the CD to totally appreciate this story.

Even though we're making the album in the summer, the memories of eighteen previous Christmases hover over me. The work we do and the tunes we make once again point me to a familiar place. I see home in every chorus, and my family and friends in every verse.

It's a cool thing to see snapshots of your life when you're singing the songs that have meant so much to you over the years.

O HOLY NIGHT

Waking up without having to be nudged. Waiting with my sister until it's time to head down the stairs to get our presents. Seeing Ashley open the presents wrapped in green, while I open the ones in red. The occasional Christmas snow seen on the ground outside. Switching between grand-parents' houses every year. Those big meals. All the decorations Mom has been putting out for several months—the decorations that are stored in their very own Christmas closet on the second floor of our home.

These are my initial memories of Christmas. I remember receiving my first guitar one Christmas from my grandpa. Just holding it in my hand made me feel so grown-up. I wanted to play it all day long. When nobody looked, I'd strike Elvis poses with it. Then I'd do the same when someone was looking.

This annual time with family to feast and have fun is always a joy. But it's not just a "holiday" for us. It's not just about Santa and his reindeer and all those presents. We're celebrating the very Person this holiday is named after, something that seems to get missed as each year passes—with holiday tunes and shopping starting in August and doubling-down on the day after Thanksgiving and then going absolutely berserk the day after Christmas.

Making an album isn't meant to fill an already flooded market with one more product to buy; it's to share the story of Jesus Christ's birth.

Those favorite Christmas tunes like "Let It Snow" and "Santa Claus Is Back in Town" are fun and full of so much joy and memories. But songs like "Mary, Did You Know?" are an opportunity to remind us why we're celebrating this day in the first place.

"Did you know that your Baby Boy has come to make you new?" the song goes. "This Child that you delivered will soon deliver you."

Every Christmas Eve before we went to bed, my family would gather around the brightly lit tree and read the Christmas story from Luke.

It really is the best story. Like when the angel comes to the young girl and gives her some pretty incredible news:

> The angel said to her, "Do not be afraid, Mary; you have found favor with God. You will con-ceive and give birth to a son, and you are to call him Jesus. He will be great and will be called the Son of the Most High. The Lord God will give him the throne of his father David, and he will reign over Jacob's descen-dants forever; his kingdom will never end."
>
> *Luke 1:30–33*

A baby born in a manger. It can end up sounding like a Hallmark card or a background carol until you begin to reflect on it and celebrate it, like the angels did after Jesus was born.

"Glory to God in the highest heaven, and on earth peace to those on whom his favor rests" (Luke 2:14).

Christmas is the *best* time to sing, especially when the lyrics have such powerful meanings.

"Born is the King of Israel."

The very reason to have Christmas in the first place. In a world full of darkness and despair, the holiday is far better than a great country song because of what it brings.

"A thrill of hope, the weary world rejoices."

My goal with a set of Christmas tunes is to be able to share some of that hope for this weary world. We all certainly need it.

THE GREATEST GIFT

Imagine an eight-year-old girl named Mugaba, with eyes far brighter than most in situations like the one she's in. But for this young Ugandan girl, she doesn't know anything different. Mugaba wants very little, simply because she lives with little. The things she wants are the things we forget we even have.

Then one day, picture Mugaba receiving something unexpected. A Christmas gift in the form of a gift-wrapped shoe box. She opens it to find personalized presents from a stranger living overseas. The name of the giver is on the box— Tessa. Inside she finds a heart-shaped necklace. A stuffed panda. A coloring set. A pink toothbrush and toothpaste. A Taylor Swift T-shirt. Colorful bracelets. A small cross. A picture of a pretty brown-haired girl who must be the one sending the presents. Then a letter written to her.

Dear Mugaba:
I hope you like the things in this box. Me and my sisters like to play with pandas so I gave you one just like ours. This necklace is something I saw and thought you'd like. This cross is something I got at church. I hope you have a Merry Christmas!
Love, Tessa

This will be the first present Mugaba has ever received. Each item will be forever significant to her.

It's crazy to think that a simple shoe box stuffed with small goodies can be met with such joy and promise. But this is exactly what Operation Christmas Child does every year. Samaritan's Purse has been doing this since 1993. That ministry provides much-needed assistance in the United States and overseas to victims of natural disaster, disease, war, and famine. Operation

Christmas Child delivers shoes boxes to children in developing countries in order to spread the message about Jesus Christ.

Along with the shoe box comes a booklet called "The Greatest Gift," which features a colorful presentation of the gospel in their own language. The boys and girls are invited to enroll in "The Greatest Journey," a twelve-lesson discipleship program. The kids end up learning from trained local volunteers what it means to follow Christ and how to share that faith with others.

This isn't a ministry I found after being on *American Idol*. Our family has been involved with it since I was very young. The great thing after winning *Idol* has been the awareness I've been able to help bring to the ministry. I was even able to go to the Dominican Republic during Christmastime 2011 to deliver hundreds of these boxes to kids.

I'd won *Idol* and had seen thousands of smiles, but these were different. The smiles on these children seemed to mirror the same kind that might be found on every corner in heaven. The yelling, screaming, and shouts of joy were so much better than the ones I've heard while singing.

There's a difference between cheering for someone and cheering for hope.

The idea behind Operation Christmas Child is as beautiful as the kids who receive the boxes.

It's so simple and easy, yet it's so very meaning-ful.

Is this a plug for Samaritan's Purse? Yes, absolutely. I can't think of a better organization to mention (*www.samaritanspurse.org*). We have so much. *I've* been given so much. A shoe box seems so ridiculously small, yet we all know the most special gifts don't always have to be the biggest. Hope and joy can come in something small and precious. Like a shoe box. Or like a newborn baby who can fit inside it.

How cool is it that we have such an easy and awesome way to show joy and hope every Christmas?

CHRISTMAS IN HEAVEN

The great songs, the special ones, end up being beloved because they help tell somebody's story or sum up an experience. They can be simple and straightforward, but sometimes they just stick. "Christmas in Heaven" is one such song. The story surrounding it is even more beautiful than the tune itself.

I'm writing a song called "Christmas in Heaven" the week before this song is sent to me. Seriously. The song I was writing was about my grandfather and how I wondered what it was like to spend Christmas in heaven. The next week, our music minister, Beth Hunnicutt, was attending a LifeWay music conference in North Carolina. Knowing we were working on a Christmas album, we told Beth that if she heard anything cool, she should send it our way. The song she sent was "Christmas in Heaven."

Sometimes you can know what you want to say, but it still takes others to articulate it, whether it's through a melody or through words.

Jeremy Johnson and Paul Marino wrote "Christmas in Heaven." Their song was exactly what I wanted to say and how I wanted to say it. They were excited when they learned that summer I'd be putting it on my upcoming holiday album.

Scotty's music helped get me through a tough time. My husband was a huge fan of Scotty. In early 2012, he was diagnosed with untreatable cancer and given only a few months to live. The day my precious husband passed away, I received Scotty's Christmas album, which I had preordered. Imagine, a few days later, when I heard "Christmas in Heaven" from his album. Number of shows I've seen? Thirty-three and counting!

REGINA ESPY,
McCREERIAN FROM ALABAMA

Months later, Jeremy and his wife, Maribeth, discovered they were pregnant. What should have been joyous news turned tragic when they learned at seventeen weeks into the pregnancy their baby had a rare chromosomal disorder called trisomy 13. The doctors told them they probably wouldn't see their child born alive. They named their baby Abbie Ann and knew God had given her to them for a reason.

Abbie Ann was born two weeks before her due date. Jeremy and Maribeth had a moving memorial service for their daughter with friends and family.

Our music minister who found the song shared the Johnsons' story at church, so my family and I were among the many prayer warriors. I'm able to meet them at the Ryman after I sing "Christmas in Heaven" during a December appearance at the Opry.

Jeremy and Maribeth share their beautiful story on YouTube, not only encouraging those in similar situations and bringing awareness to trisomy 13, but also ministering to anyone who feels shattered and beyond hope. Their testimony is something amazing to see, and it's one I'd rather you dis-cover fully on your own, reading it in their own moving words.

Sometimes you write a verse asking a simple question: "Are you singing with angels, 'Silent Night'?"

Sometimes someone can hear that song and feel it speaking to them and reminding them of a lost loved one.

Sometimes the very words you once wrote can suddenly become a story you're living.

Our lives are all part of God's never-ending story of hope and love. The songs worth writing and singing are about how we handle the dark moments we inevitably find ourselves in.

Jeremy and Maribeth Johnson are two shining reflections of a song written before God gave them Abbie Ann. If anybody doesn't believe that songs are gifts given to the songwriter, then all you have to do is listen to "Christmas in Heaven."

I'm privileged to have been able to share their gift with others.

But that's what Christmas is all about, right?

THE CENTERPIECE

Every year, my mom puts out the same holiday tablecloth that will be used for the whole month of December. Since 1988, that tablecloth has been used as a canvas for memories and messages written in permanent marker by family and friends. Each year, there are a few more words, names, and stories added to the faded cloth.

In some ways, this tablecloth reminds me of a

country singer. To be honest, it kinda reminds me of myself. Every year, I'm able to share fragments of my life. Pieces of joy, fun, and thankfulness. Instead of messages written down in markers, I'm able to sing and record songs. They're the same thing, however—permanent memories that aren't going to go away.

My first album, my Christmas CD, my follow-ups to them. This book. The concerts . . .

They're all scribbles on a tablecloth. Memories and messages in the form of music. Catchy reminders of hope and promise.

At the center resides the same focal point of the Christmas holiday.

"For God so loved the world that he gave his one and only Son, that whoever believes in him shall not perish but have eternal life" (John 3:16).

Chapter Ten

The Thrill and the Joy (of Sports)

My first gig was pitching. Baseball was always a huge part of my life. It's something I always practiced, something my father helped instill a love for and then helped me grow in as an athlete. Music, on the other hand, was always a passion.

So naturally, my love of sports doesn't go away after I win *Idol.* Think about the show for a moment. It's a competition, right? I was singing *and* competing. That's a perfect combination for me.

My love of the game, whether baseball, football, golf, or anything, stays with me even as the music opportunities keep coming. In the same way I'm determined to finish high school and go to college, I also make a choice to play baseball and continue following my favorite passion— music.

With my newfound fame, I'll realize this will be a blessing and a curse. That goes all the way back to my senior year as I played baseball on my school team for my last season.

CURVEBALLS

I step onto the pitcher's mound and feel a sense of both relief and panic. Lots of eyes are watching me, quite a few more than the last time I was here. It's been more than a year and a half since I've been able to pitch for the Garner Trojans. There's something I'm feeling on this warm March day. It's not confidence or strength or determination.

No.

It's a case of the nerves.

The news crew that showed up an hour before the game should've been expected. I knew the word would get out I was pitching today. But still—a part of me just wants to be a small-town high school senior pitching in his first game of the season. That's all. But now I have the lens of a camera watching me.

You should be used to it by now.

I am. But that doesn't mean I'm not wired and anxious.

I look into the dugout at my teammates. There have been some benefits from me having ventured out on the *Idol* express. One of those is being able to buy the team new warm-up jackets. I'm eighteen and have earned some money, so it's a cool thing to be able to do. But I'm not sure they think all the press our team is getting this year is so cool.

I compose myself, take a breath, and let out what feels like my very first pitch. Ever.

I throw a curveball. It feels good. I know it before I hear it.

"Strike one."

There's more applause than usual. I guess that's a good thing. I know my parents and Ash are in the stands. Once again, I know I'm causing them great stress.

It takes two more curveballs to strike the batter out.

Not bad for a rusty country singer.

When the inning is all said and done, I struck out two and didn't allow any runs or hits.

In the end, we don't win the game, but it's not about how well Scotty McCreery did. I'm a team player, and that's what matters. I'm grateful to be suiting up with my friends, playing for my school, and still being cheered on by my home-town.

DON'T BE CRUEL

"Stick to singing, McCreery," the opposing team yells from their dugout.

Ah, yes. Now the guys I'm playing against have a lot more ammunition when it comes to talking junk.

I'm at another home game, and the comments are coming from the opposing team's dugout. After more trash talk, one of my best friends leaps to my defense. Alec Hulmes is our first baseman, and he's not about to listen to these guys mouthing off about me.

Every time they yell, he dishes it right back. The goading continues.

"Where's the number to call and vote?"

"Hey, baby, why don't you lock them doors!"

"Randy Jackson called, and he said you suck."

Alec continues to talk back at them, but I can't exactly share all the things he says. I'll sum it up by saying he's not really fond of their comments.

Not long after this game, we play an away game and get a win. After the game is over, the teams line up and walk across the mound to shake hands. One of the other team's players comes up and shakes my hand with a tight grip and a mean-looking grin.

"Your music sucks," he says.

I nod and smile. "Appreciate you listenin', brother."

He really doesn't like that reply.

Most of my harassment, however, comes from the guys I'm playing with. It's a good thing 'cause it keeps me humble. Sometimes they'll mention something about my singing, and other times they'll just rib me like they always have. It's all in good fun and no different than before.

A BRIEF SCARE

There's a memorable moment during that senior baseball season. It's when I get hit by a ball.

In the throat.

It's the third inning when a ground ball takes a funny hop and lands squarely below my jaw. I finish the play, throwing the ball to first and getting the batter out. Then I toss my glove to the ground and grab my throat. I walk off the mound toward the outfield. I don't say anything at first.

If you're a guy who wants a career as a singer, this is about the worst place to take a hit.

I compose myself as the coach comes out to check on me.

"He got me in the moneymaker," I tell him with a chuckle.

I hum a bit and can hear that familiar sound, so I know I'm good. It's a little sting, and a far bigger scare. I'm glad music hasn't affected my ability to compete in sports. But this game made me realize sports could affect my ability to sing.

THE WOLFPACK

I remember talking to the head baseball coach at NC State about trying out for the team. I know it's a long shot, but why not just have the conversation? Coach Elliott Avent, who at one time was my dad's assistant coach in college, tells me I

> Scotty loves his NC State Wolfpack more than any fan of any team I have ever known. It's not uncommon to be watching a game together (of any sport) and hear him say, "See that guy right there, his uncle—guess where he played?" After four and a half years together, I still shake my head because I know the answer: NC State. Every. Time.
>
> JOEY SANCHEZ, DRUMMER

have a Division I slider but a Division IV fastball, a combo that doesn't quite offer the variety they're looking for.

The competitive part of me considers this.

Maybe if I start training and working hard, I can get on the team.

This is quite a big "if." And that's if *all* I happened to be doing was attending college. But I'm writing music, recording music, *and* touring.

There's no way.

Sometimes you have to bring a little reality into a situation when it comes to your dreams. So while I don't get to play sports at NC State, I still will forever be a part of the Wolfpack and share a whole host of favorite memories related to their teams.

Memories like watching Philip Rivers make his debut as our quarterback in 2000 and getting a win in double overtime against Arkansas State. Each week, Rivers seemed to grow. By his junior year, Rivers led our team to nine consecutive victories, finishing off the year by beating Notre Dame in the Gator Bowl. By the end of his senior year, Rivers had started fifty-one straight games and finished his collegiate career with an insane number of honors and records.

How could I not be excited when Rivers was drafted into the NFL? I still root for him. That is, when his San Diego Chargers aren't playing my Patriots.

Over the years I've fallen in love with and rooted for many Wolfpack teams and players. Football players like Russell Wilson, Mario Williams, and Mike Glennon. Basketball players like Julius Hodge, T. J. Warren, and Scott Wood.

Watching the Wolfpack play while I'm on the road or when I'm home has become part of my life. Not long ago, I got a chance to storm the basketball court after NC State won. I had been sitting next to our football coach, Dave Doeren, and his eight-year-old son, so I invite the boy to come with me.

"He better not," the coach tells me.

"Aw, he'll be fine," I say. "I'll keep him at my side."

So Doeren's son and I head into the crowd that's as crazy as a—oh, come on, I have to say it—pack of wolves. I'm celebrating and cheering and high-fiving, and all of a sudden, I look down and realize his son is missing.

Uh-oh.

Five minutes after saying everything will be fine, I've lost the coach's second grade son. It's only for a few brief moments, but still . . .

I might be an ideal fan, but I sure need some lessons in babysitting.

RED SOX AND PATRIOTS

We inherit many things from our parents. Sometimes it's in our genes; other times it's in our passions.

Since my dad grew up in Maine, one definite thing he gave me was a love for New England sports teams.

My fifth grade journal shares my love of those teams even back then:

I Love It When the Red Sox Beat the Yankees

I love it when the Red Sox beat the Yankees. I am a big RED SOX FAN. I hate the Yankees. I have a feeling one day when I am living the RED SOX will break the curse and win the world series. I have a feeling the Yankees will have a huge slump. I have to admit the

Yankees have some good players. But I down right hate the Yankees. That is why I love it when the Red Sox beat the Yankees.

GO SOX!

Looking back at this exquisite piece of prose, we can see several things.

1. I love it when the Red Sox beat the Yankees.
2. I can predict the future.
3. I hate the Yankees.
4. I really love it when the Red Sox beat the Yankees.

Later that year, I wrote a song based on my other favorite team.

New England Patriots

12/1/04

We've got two and you've got none.
Ha ha ha ha ha ha.
We're gonna make it three this year.
Ha ha ha ha ha ha.
We're on the road to a world record.
Ha ha ha ha ha ha.
~~Come you know we are the Patriots my friends~~
~~—Ohh Yeahhh~~

(drums) bum bum bum, bum bum ba bum
    bum
Pattrriioottss—bum bum bum, bum bum ba
    bum bum
Superbowl bum bum bum, bum bum ba bum
    bum
Champions (pause)
We're the best team in football (repeat)
Those Panthers had a lucky season (repeat)
Those Titans sure can't bring us down (repeat)
Those Steelers stole our victory (repeat)

CHAMPIONS

As you can see, my songwriting in fifth grade was already well developed. In fact, I've been trying to cut this song for years now.

Are you reading this, Mr. Kraft?

I did indeed write that, and my love for the Patriots has only grown. How could it not?

Again, this piece shows I can predict the future. It also shows I sure like to talk smack, right?

SUPER BOWL

I have reasons to root for both teams playing in Super Bowl XLIX on February 1, 2015. The starting quarterback for the Seattle Seahawks is Russell Wilson, a former NC State Wolfpack guy.

They're playing New England, however, so there's no debate whatsoever who I'll be rooting for. I hope Russell has a good game. But not too good.

Dad and I head to Arizona early so I can sing at the Patriots pre–Super Bowl party on Thursday night. I'm able to meet the owner of the Patriots, Robert Kraft. Hopefully I'm bringing Mr. Kraft and the team some good, *American Idol*–winning vibes.

As far as Super Bowls go, this has to be one of the greatest ever played. I know I'm biased. This one is decided in the closing seconds.

Coach Pete Carroll of the Seahawks has already been a gambling man today. At the end of the second quarter, right before halftime, Carroll calls a play from scrimmage instead of kicking a field goal to get closer to the Patriots, who are leading 14–7. With six seconds on the clock, Russell Wilson throws a pass for a touchdown.

In the second half, the Patriots fall behind 24–14, so they have to go all-out Brady to pull ahead again. Brady throws two touchdown passes to put the Patriots ahead 28–24. Soon the clock is ticking down, and Dad and I get to see firsthand what the rest of the world sees on television.

One eye-popping unlikely catch and one mind-exploding play call.

The stadium seems to shake as the closing

Scotty and I attended the Super Bowl to watch the Patriots beat Seattle. The way the game ended was so dramatic that while we were celebrating, Scotty asked me to hoist him up on my shoulders. Here is my twenty-one-year-old on top of his dad's shoulders, celebrating a Super Bowl win. It's a moment I will never forget.

MIKE McCREERY

minute of the game approaches. I know we just have to hang on and not let them score. But then I see Wilson launch a ball to his wide receiver, Jermaine Kearse.

No no no no no no.

The ball hangs up there as Kearse and a rookie cornerback named Malcolm Butler run downfield, reaching the ten yard line before both go for the ball. Butler launches himself in front of the wide receiver and barely deflects the pass. The ball drops and *bounces* on Kearse, who then somehow scoops it up for the catch.

I honestly can't breathe.

At the time, I'm wanting to believe it's not a catch. It surely can't be a catch. There's no way he caught that ball.

Yeah, he did, and they're going to win. Is that Russell Wilson or Eli Manning?

I feel like I'm going to be sick.

Seeing it on the big screen confirms it. So the Seahawks have first and goal on the five yard line with sixty-five seconds left to play.

Dad and I are in a state of complete shock, just like the rest of Patriots Nation.

The great Seahawk running back, Marshawn Lynch, runs the ball to the one yard line, taking some precious time off the clock.

Second down and goal, with twenty-six seconds left to play.

It's over.

So Coach Carroll decides to go big or go home. That's right. He makes a gutsy call and decides to pass the ball. The throw is a quick slant pass. The Patriots rookie cornerback has done his home-work and studied the tape, so he's ready. The ball ends up in the steady hands of Malcolm Butler.

Our Malcolm Butler.

Patriots ball.

Go big or go home, right? I still love my Wolfpack guy Russell, but it looks like the Seahawks are going home. The rest of the sports world will be screaming about the play that will live on in infamy. Lots and lots of people will be calling it the worst play call ever.

Dad and I think it was a pretty awesome call ourselves.

SIDE BY SIDE

As the plane's engine hums, I look out the window and see a sprawling green landscape below us. It's a lush green like I've never seen, reminding me of the Emerald City. We have the Augusta National Golf Club in sight. In just a short time, my father and I will be teeing off and playing on the same course where golf's most prestigious tournament, the Masters, has been held since 1934.

I'm a decent golfer, but my father has spent his whole life playing the sport. He used to golf all the time with his father. Granddaddy Bill loved to golf. After my granddad retired from the Air Force and later from the civil service, he joined Cochecho Country Club in Dover, New Hampshire. My father played there four or five times a week as a teenager. When Dad wasn't playing, he worked in the pro shop. He later became the assistant pro at the course. Granddaddy Bill and Grandma Paquita would eventually retire and move to Pinehurst, North Carolina, a town not too far from Garner. They would become members at the famous Pinehurst Golf Resort.

Through my record label, my father and I have this amazing chance to golf at Augusta National. The weather is perfect. I have new clubs. Everything feels right.

Then I start to have one of the most terrible games of my life. Sure, it's Augusta. But still, it's frustrating.

I don't make a single par for the first eleven holes. Then we arrive at the twelfth hole: Golden Bell.

This is the same No. 12 that the great Jack Nicklaus said featured the toughest tee shot on the entire course. His amazing round of 30 on the back nine at Augusta in 1986 allowed him to win the Masters, but it did feature one bogey.

Golden Bell.

They say it's the wind on this hole that plays with golfers' minds. The wind doesn't matter on this day, however. I'm already shanking and hooking and chunking.

The fight in me is always there, even though I may appear calm and nonchalant on the outside. I always try my best, always hope to win, and always keep playing.

My first shot lands just short of the green and promptly rolls back into Rae's Creek. After taking my drop, I pull out my pitching wedge, hoping to just get the ball close to the hole to make another bogey. Instead, it's a perfect chip shot that rolls into the cup.

A par has never felt so triumphant.

I can see my father wearing a big grin on his face. Both of us are in a state of disbelief. Of course, we've been in a state of disbelief before, so this is nothing new. But it sure does feel good. Mastering one of golf's greatest holes!

There's something magical about walking around Augusta National, a course that so many greats in golf have played. It gives you a greater appreciation for the difficulty of the game and the beauty of the sport. Like so many things, you can't fully understand and appreciate something until you journey through it with your own two feet.

My father—this steady and confident guide in my life from the day I was born—walks alongside me over these fairways. His love of the game has given me so much. Not just a love of golf, but a love of competition. His quiet but fierce sports-manship has always been on display, and it's been something I've tried to emulate.

Those weeks on *Idol* when I'd be working hard to make it to the next round resemble these holes we're playing now. They're difficult, and few get to compete on them. So winning is something special indeed.

For me, there's such a thrill and joy in playing and watching sports. On this glorious day, I'm thankful to once again have my father at my side to share the experience.

Chapter Eleven

ASAP—Always Say a Prayer

I've learned in this short but very full life that sometimes things happen to make you stop in your tracks. Maybe there's no explanation, no burning bush to spell out why God allows something to happen. Except maybe, possibly, it's to press the pause button for a moment. To catch your breath and stay in place.

And maybe even appreciate the fact that you can breathe in the first place.

KEEP THEM DOORS LOCKED

"Strength and honor."

These are the words General Maximus Decimus Meridius shares at the start of the epic movie *Gladiator* starring Russell Crowe. He speaks these words moments before the Roman army goes out to battle the Germanic tribes one last, blood-drenched time. The men are filing in place, getting ready to rush at one another in the middle of a fire-ravaged forest.

Our hero rides his horse and then delivers a

memorable speech that makes me want to follow him into battle.

"Three weeks from now, I will be harvesting my crops. Imagine where you will be, and it will be so."

Fear and the sense of dread mix with a triumphant, determined spirit.

"Hold the line! Stay with me! If you find yourself alone, riding in the green fields with the sun on your face, do not be troubled. For you are in Elysium, and you're already dead!"

There is nervous laughter from his cavalry. Then Maximus continues.

"Brothers, what we do in life . . . echoes in eternity."

That's the moment we hear the knocking on the apartment door.

It's close to 2:00 a.m., and I'm hanging out with some buddies from NC State after getting a bite to eat at Cook Out. We're watching the movie and then hear a knock on the door. None of us think anything of it.

I should be sleeping by now. Honestly. I opened for Lady Antebellum last night in Pelham, Alabama, on their Take Me Downtown tour. I haven't been a part of this tour, but the date had been rescheduled at the Oak Mountain Amphitheatre. They needed an opener for the new date, and I was available. After the show, I spent the night in Birmingham and planned to fly back to

Raleigh the next morning on a six o'clock flight.

A plane delay that morning forced me to drive a rental car to Atlanta, where I missed another plane. I finally get back to North Carolina around 6:00 p.m. after having been up since 4:00 a.m.

One of the guys living at the apartment gets up from the couch, assuming the knock on the door is from one of their neighbors. He looks through the peephole and sees a guy who doesn't look suspicious, so he opens it, thinking someone must have a question or a problem.

That's when all hell breaks loose and enters the living room where we're sitting.

Four guys barge in waving guns. Real guns that mean real business. The first guy carries an assault rifle and puts it up against my friend's sternum. The other two are carrying pistols. They shout their demands right away.

"Get down! Get on the floor and give us everything you got!"

There are shouts, screams, and curses. My friends are saying, "Who are you? What are you doing here?"

It's not long before I feel the barrel of a pistol against my forehead.

This is real and raw, and I'm thinking I'm going to die any second.

I had experienced a similar fear on a visit to London on July 7, 2005. My dad, who had traveled to Europe several times for business, was finally taking our family overseas for the first time. After experiencing the northern part of England, we were driving into London when we saw mysterious signs on the highway that read, "Avoid London. Area closed. Turn on radio for further details." Since the radio didn't work in our rental car, we had no clue what was happening and drove straight to Heathrow Airport. The scene of massive chaos and policemen holding machine guns was terrifying. We were stranded at the air-port for hours as we listened to local news reports about detonated bombs in the London tube and bus system. It was strange seeing my parents genuinely afraid and helpless.

I'm feeling the same way with a gun pressed against me.

"Whatever you want, take it," I say.

The thought of these guys recognizing me fills me with absolute horror. Months earlier, I had performed for more than fifty thousand people a few miles from here on Hillsborough Street at NC State's Packapalooza. Do they recognize my voice? Do they recognize me in my shorts, Wolfpack cap, and T-shirt?

The good news is they don't. Maybe I'm just looking a bit too normal for them to think any-thing about me. Maybe they've been too busy being thugs to keep track of Season 10 of *American Idol*. I don't know, and I don't care. I just want them gone.

My mind flashes back to a local news story a few years earlier. In Chapel Hill, just thirty miles away, the UNC student body president was kidnapped from her apartment in the early hours of the morning. She was forced to withdraw money from an ATM and was later shot and killed on a Chapel Hill Street.

"Please, God," I pray, "don't let them kidnap us."

If they *had* known who I was, I'd be in a lot of trouble. I had a new PIN number for my debit card, and I'd forgotten it. Wouldn't that sound like a complete lie? Even *I* wouldn't believe it. Standing with me at an ATM—a gun still aimed at my head, me truthfully not being able to get any money out—they would have gotten mad, and who knows what would have happened next. Thankfully, nobody recognizes me.

Of all the things these guys could have taken, all they end up with are a few wallets, my buddy's laptop, some electronics, and some phones—including mine. Eventually, we call the cops and then our families.

In the end, one of the robbers turns himself in, and two other men are suspected of being involved. Unfortunately, I have to deal with the public side, releasing a statement and sharing some thoughts on social media. Local news anchors who are family friends call for details. A Fox News truck ends up in front of our house, hoping for a statement. Eventually, I'm even calling in to the Ryan Seacrest radio show to share the experience.

Lessons learned again. The takeaway? Lock them doors. Really. And never, ever open your door at 2:00 a.m. for a stranger.

I'd be fine and content to have gone my whole life not ever feeling a gun pressed against my forehead. But God is in control, and all I can say is a very, very relieved "THANK YOU, JESUS."

RIP

It's a good thing I didn't die in that robbery. No, my passing officially occurs on April 5, 2013. At least that's what one online news report declares.

Musician Scotty McCreery died while on a personal vacation in Turks and Caicos early this morning from injuries sustained in a Jet Ski accident.

Jet skiing in Turks and Caicos? Somehow I don't remember that. Did I have fun? The news report goes on to say I had hit a boat dock and happened to be the only person on the Jet Ski. Then it ends by saying they didn't yet have "specific details" about the accident.

Good thing those *specific* details aren't available. No, just the fuzzy, false kind. I first hear about this when I see some online chatter in tweets that ask, "Is @ScottyMcCreery really dead?" and "I can't believe Scotty's dead!" In a way, however, it's a twisted sort of honor, since lots of big-name celebrities have been pranked in that way. And actually, on the very same day the word is spreading on my demise, the same news (probably from the same jokesters) is circulating about Blake Shelton being killed in a car accident.

Well, the boys 'round here are still around, thank God. I love a good Jet Ski, but I'll probably avoid one if I'm ever in Turks and Caicos. Just in case.

A SAD SONG

Many people have argued whether or not Elvis Presley's longtime manager, Colonel Tom Parker, took him for a ride by taking lots more money than he should have. After Elvis died, his estate was worth around ten million dollars, though he'd earned over a billion dollars during his career. Even with the fifty-fifty split with his manager, something seemed very fishy.

The list of managers who didn't do right by their musician clients is quite long. Sometimes artists are fortunate to find someone they can work with and trust. Like the way I was fortunate to find Mike and my band and crew.

As far as a manager goes—well, there are

some bumps on that business road, though I don't believe I've ever been taken for a ride quite like that. It's rare for an artist to have only one manager for their entire career. The key, however, is keeping the change low-drama. This was one of those learning lessons for me. A very public one, in fact.

I was without a manager in 2012 when Todd Cassetty approached me. Todd did video work for Hi-Fi Fusion in Nashville. When he found out I had no manager, he flew to North Carolina to pitch himself, telling us how educated he was and calling current Nashville managers the "dinosaur club." He had never been a manager but had done some video work for me. My mom adored him, and we all believed he could do some cool things.

I decide to give him a shot, and Todd has a public relations friend issue a press release that November to all of Nashville about his new company and an *American Idol* winner becoming his first client.

A few months later, the following March, I feel it's time to part ways. That's long enough to realize something's just not working. Then, when I realize Todd hasn't stepped away from his current business, I *know* it's time to part ways. As my attorney said during this time, you can't steal second if your foot is still on first. The reality here is I'm running a business. A large, multimillion-dollar business with a team of valuable, talented, and trusted people.

I had already been paying Todd's expenses and had given him a Christmas bonus. Those items, plus the settlement I offer, brings things to almost six figures, which I think is fair for the few months he was on board. Well, he feels he's owed hundreds of thousands more. He has Stephen Zralek and Ed Yarbrough of Bone Law proceed to sue me for $570,000. Really? Wow.

Look, Ronnie Milsap sang "nobody likes sad songs," and I agree. Especially if they're from some young, deeply blessed singer lamenting a lawsuit over money. I'm just sharing a very major life lesson for a guy who at that time had only been in the industry two years.

There are two sides here, and I'm not talking about a plaintiff and a defendant; I'm talking about art and business. There's this love of harmony, riffs, and hearing the fiddle play. Then there's the hunger for dollar signs and commas separating numbers. Lots and lots of numbers.

You idolize an iconic singer and you spend your life imitating him. Then one day, you find yourself stepping out into that light, only to see it embrace you. But the other side of that light is darkness. A cold, dark side where people with quick smiles and "attaboys" stand ready to use your talent to fill their wallets.

I would have loved to settle out of court, but

Todd's camp never proposes a reasonable offer. The lawsuit turns into a court case to determine what to pay this guy. It's not a matter of winning or losing, since I already offered to pay him. Of course, that doesn't stop someone from issuing a story to the Nashville press saying Todd had won.

There's a big learning curve for me, along with some truly head-scratching moments. But it is what it is.

I issue a statement saying all I want to say about this matter. How I'd offered to pay him more than once, but his request for compensation for his services was beyond what seemed fair.

"While it has been difficult to risk having my reputation challenged, I always believed the truth would prevail, and it has," my press release states. Five of the six claims Todd and his

---

Having worked with Garth, Trisha, Paisley, Frampton, and many others, I'm not easily impressed. However, when I first experienced Scotty's charming manner and observed his respectful way of interacting with everyone, from fans to journalists, I began to realize I wanted to work with this guy. Three years later, he asked me to be part of his team. Best invitation ever.

SCOTT STEM, PUBLICIST

---

attorney, Mr. Zralek, filed against me are dismissed or dropped. VICTORY. Todd is awarded less than half of what he asks. ANOTHER VICTORY.

But the story doesn't end there. From the beginning, we felt the tone of the whole ordeal was a money grab (my attorney's words), as well as a campaign to attack me so Todd could save face. I mean, the original complaint was so nasty. Because we are convinced some items in the initial complaint are not based on solid facts, my attorney files a Rule 11 motion against Zralek of Bone Law. We feel he has pushed the envelope and should be sanctioned. The judge rules for him, yet we're thankful the legal system allowed us to address our concerns.

At the age of twenty, I'm having to issue official press statements about being sued. Have mercy. How much drama can one guy take? Where's the guidebook for this business? One thing is certain: When there's a problem, follow the dollar.

I'm just a guy who wants to sing. But that guy is learning not everyone is worried about the singing part. Some are only interested in what the singing might bring their way.

Yes, I'm learning every day. I've worked with a lot of great people who really care about me. But this episode taught me that to some, I'm just a dollar sign. So I'm learning to be careful about everything and everyone who comes my way.

ASAP

I learn a lot from a bus driver we spend a summer with. His name is W.C., and he's one of the coolest guys I've ever met. I sit up late in the folding seat at the very front of the bus, listening to him tell incredible stories.

I'll admit it—I've gotten a bit tough to impress. Not because of anything bad but because of all the things that have happened to me over the years. But W.C. keeps impressing me with tale after tale.

He had a tough childhood. His father abandoned him, and he was a member of a gang in New York. He was a talented athlete, however, and he eventually earned a spot on the basketball team at NC State. W.C. played during the David Thompson years. NC State is where he met his wife.

He drove for people who were much more famous than me. A lady named Oprah Winfrey. A poet named Maya Angelou. A band called Led Zeppelin.

If that's not enough, he also happens to be Kobe Bryant's uncle.

W.C. doesn't just share the experiences he's had; he gives me advice on how to run my business. He stresses again and again the importance of saving money. "You better stack that paper, Wolfpack kid," he would tell me in his deep, soulful voice. The celebrities took very good care of W.C., but at the same time, he took very good care of them.

At the core of all his stories is one thing. And perhaps this is why I listen to him as attentively as I do. Perhaps this is why he impresses me so much. He is a man of great faith, a man who teaches me a saying. It's a saying that can go with anything—nervousness before going onstage, worries about a business deal, or a gun being pressed against my forehead.

"ASAP," W.C. says. "Always say a prayer."

More than anything else, it's important to always say a prayer.

"God will give you the strength," W.C. tells me. "You just gotta ask Him."

STILL HERE

The last lines of *Gladiator* are uttered by one of the slaves who fought alongside Maximus. Juba says this about his slain friend: "I will see you again . . . but not yet . . . not yet."

Sometimes I feel like I tell the real world this often. The regular world, the world of people working nine to five and coming home to a house and a family. Sleeping in a familiar bed instead of a bunk on a bus. Having a boss and getting the weekends off and occasionally finding themselves fighting off boredom. Believe me, I love what I do. And I signed up for a life on the road, but to stay grounded and sane, I need to connect with the real, everyday world I came from.

I think of the real world and I say, "I will see you again.

"But not yet . . . not yet."

Chapter Twelve

On the Road

I'm singing the Travis Tritt song "T-R-O-U-B-L-E" at a concert in Bethel, New York, and I'm into it. The band is jammin', and I'm channeling my inner Tritt. I'm moving and singing and getting the crowd ready for Brad Paisley, who comes on later.

"Well a sweet talkin', sexy walkin', honky—"

Suddenly I'm free-falling into the crowd. Thankfully I don't land headfirst on the ground. Instead I land in a pretty lady's lap. I give her a nod and a "hey, how ya doin'" and then balance myself and get back onto the platform. I find her during Brad's encore and give her an autographed picture for enduring a 170-pound belly flop mid-concert. It may be the first time but certainly not the last time I launch myself off the stage into someone or something.

While I keep singing, a little seed of a big prank is planted.

An hour later, after the band has the gear loaded offstage and we're back in the dressing room, we come up with a plan. The victim is going to be one of my tech guys, Jori Johnson.

The first time I saw Jori in rehearsals after he'd

been hired by Jayme and Mike, I had some serious doubts. He was lanky and quiet, with blue hair that looked like it belonged to a cast member from a *Twilight* movie.

This guy isn't going to last.

As it turns out, Jori would definitely last and become an invaluable part of our team. The guy does everything. *Everything.* He works 24/7. He's the first one up and the last one to go to bed (outside of our merchandise guy, Carson). Jori is also the nicest guy in the world. So early on, we simply wanted to help him feel like part of the team. And the way our band shows that is by abusing each other.

Let's call it tough love.

By the time Jori comes into the dressing room, the plan is already hatched. He opens the door, and I storm out of there.

"I'll be on the bus," I say, trying to sound irritated.

I can do Elvis, but it's hard to do irate.

Everybody else follows me, except Mike and Matt. We have our phones hidden in the room, recording everything, so we're able to see later what all went down.

Jori is wondering what's up until Mike begins to talk with him in a stern tone.

"Jori, I know you saw Scotty fall off the stage tonight," Mike says. "So according to Bill, the stage is narrower than it usually is. Bill said he told you to let me know. Jori, why didn't you tell me about that? Is that true?"

Bill is Brad's stage manager, and trust me, you want to stay on his good side. He runs a tight ship and doesn't hold back. Jori gives Mike a look of both confusion and terror. We're outside the dressing room, holding back our laughter while we listen to the conversation.

Jori shakes his head. "Man, I don't think so—I mean, maybe. I don't know."

Mike is putting on an Academy Award–winning performance.

"So, Jori, look—fortunately Scotty's not hurt," Mike tells him. "His pride is bruised. He just fell in front of fourteen thousand people. You can imagine how he might feel."

Mike's completely selling it, and the poor kid is totally buying it.

"Listen, Jori. It really comes down to a communication issue," Mike tells him.

We're all listening and dying, but poor, sweet, happy-go-lucky Jeff can't take the abuse any longer.

"Guys," he says in a whisper, "let's don't do this anymore."

Our production manager, Jayme, starts radioing to Jori, telling him we need him outside.

"I can't really come now," Jori says, probably thinking he might be fired.

"No, Jori, I need you right now," Jayme says.

Eventually he comes out and sees us in the hallway and knows he's being messed with. We all jump him and share a big laugh.

"You never defended yourself," Mike jokingly tells the poor guy later on.

The best part comes the following night when Brad Paisley hears about it and decides to have some fun himself. When I come onstage the next evening, the stage walkway has yellow caution tape surrounding it and orange traffic cones lining the edges. I leave them up and joke with the crowd, telling them Paisley wants me to be extra cautious since I fell off the stage the night before.

Our young, hardworking, and always amiable Jori has come a long way since then. We wouldn't trade him for anything.

STOMP AND KICK

If you have to be away from your immediate family while on the road, it's good to be with your second family. That's how we feel as a band. It's a rare thing to have everybody get along; it's especially rare to have gotten along for so very long.

Picture a one-bedroom apartment for twelve people crammed into a metal tube traveling seventy miles per hour. That's what life on the road looks and feels like. Granted, occasionally we'll have two of those metal tubes, but still. We're fortunate everybody likes each other.

I've been on tours where bands have changed more members in a month than we've done in five years. A different tour manager showing up every couple weeks.

Like I've said, God has surrounded me with some good guys. A good team.

One of the key ingredients is having a good time. And good times with family mean pranks. Lots and lots of pranks.

Dylan Rosson joins our merry band of brothers early in 2014. Mike spots Dylan tearing up the guitar with Charlie Daniels at a Christian men's event I'm singing at in Nashville in late 2013. After he auditioned, we bring him on board. We're about the same age, but he looks even younger than I do, making it more unbelievable to see him play. An added bonus is he's got great vocals too. Dylan grew up not realizing there were other genres of music besides country and 1970s soft rock.

Just like many of the other guys, Dylan is at a point where his parents are forcing him to either find a regular job or come back home and start living a normal life again. Thankfully, he joins our team of people who live *not-so-normal* lives.

He's been playing with us for a couple of weeks before we decide to initiate him into our fold. We go a bit "Spinal Tap" on poor, young Dylan.

Jeff, the bandleader, does a masterful job at prepping the young guitarist during rehearsals. We tell the newcomer the plan is for the band to march together onto the stage toward the crowd, walking with ridiculous military band steps while playing. Then when we reach the edge of the stage, we will all jump.

Dylan is asking questions and trying to get the routine right.

"It's so hard for me to play and figure this stuff out," he tells our band.

Yeah, that's because it's absolute nonsense.

"I'm going to have to go home and practice this," Dylan says.

There's not just one bit we have him rehearse. Nope. We want to spread the joke over the course of the night, so there are a couple of spots we get him to practice. So the night of the show comes, and we're all ready.

For the opening song, Dylan does his military stomp march to the center of the stage while we stay back. He's into it too. Dylan does the quick jump and then looks to his side to see . . . nobody. He glances behind him as he slowly starts to shuffle back to the rest of the guys. They don't act like anything's up.

Another bit we've taught him is the high kick. As the guys come together at the front of the stage, jammin' to our cover of "That's All Right," the moment comes and boom—Dylan launches a nice karate-style boot in the air. Then he glances at Jeff with a complete look of confusion covering his youthful and naive face. Jeff and I can't hold back our laughter.

After the show, we still mess with our guitarist.

"Why would Dylan be the only one kicking?" Joey says with a complete straight face.

Seconds later, we reveal the truth, and there's instant hilarity.

"I quit!" he says as we surround him the way a team of players huddles together on a field.

He's been welcomed into our brotherhood. He's a part of us.

Heaven help the poor guy.

STANDING UP AND FITTING IN

Even before this, we know right away that Dylan fits in with our group. On one of the first days, Joey starts giving him a hard time, and Dylan fires right back.

"Wow, that's pretty brave for the new guy," Joey says.

"Listen, I know how this goes," Dylan tells him. "This is like the first day of prison. I'm either going to stand up for myself or end up being somebody's punching bag."

I might be paraphrasing his words just a little to make this conversation family friendly, but you get it. Dylan immediately fits in. So much so that it doesn't take him long to strike back at Joey where it hurts the most. Since Dylan still lives at home with his parents, we'll often joke with him about Mom still making him peanut butter and jelly sandwiches.

"But that's good, Dylan," Joey says. "Save your money. You're going to buy a house."

Dylan doesn't hesitate for a second.

"Look, Joe. I don't want to come one day and ask for your daughter's hand in marriage without being able to provide for her."

There are very few people who can bring our beloved Joey to complete silence. But Dylan, our brand-new guitarist, is the one who manages to do it.

He doesn't have to save up for a new home 'cause he's found one here.

CARSON

One of our constant sources for humor on the road is Carson, our merchandise manager. He's in

291

his sixties and has been in the business since he was, what—maybe five years old? At least it seems like it. Carson's been everywhere and seen everything.

Seriously.

He's one of those rare Nashville natives, born and raised in the town before it became what it is today. An early neighbor happened to be—get this—Willie Nelson.

Carson's the one who needs to write a book. He's a graduate of the University of Tennessee, where he played football. After playing minor league baseball and teaching school for a while, he unexpectedly got into the music business, selling T-shirts for bands and going on tour with them. The list of bands and musicians he's worked with is pretty incredible: the Rolling Stones, Pink Floyd, Kiss, Genesis, Garth, Urban, Chesney, McGraw, and many others.

By the time he got a call about working with our team, I think he was ready for a nice break from the usual tours he'd been doing. Carson was supposed to be going on tour with the Red Hot Chili Peppers when he was told about this young guy who won *American Idol*. Carson hadn't really heard of me, but he was curious. Especially when he was told I was moving lots of merchandise. Lots.

Carson didn't actually believe it until he saw it himself. My merchandise sales were ten times what they should've been. Nobody could figure out what was happening.

"I've never seen this," Carson said—and he really had seen everything.

One time, it got to a point where one of the other acts we were with on the road sent a spy to try to figure out how and why we were selling so many shirts and other things. It was unheard-of how much we were selling. A stranger actually approached me out of nowhere and sat me down.

"How are you selling so many shirts every night?" the guy asked me.

We would come to simply realize that people showed their love and support by buying lots of stuff. Carson was very happy to help them out. He was also content to be a part of our group.

Sometimes one of us in the band will go to his bunk in the bus and try to wake him up, and we'll all have the same thought.

What if . . .

Carson *is* a bit more mature than us—you know what I'm talking about. Plus, what he does *is* physically demanding and entails crazy hours. We always joke that one day we're going to nudge him awake in his bus bunk and keep nudging him until we realize maybe he's not waking up. *Ever.*

Of course, we're only joking around with Carson, but some mornings leave us wondering.

"Carson," someone will say. "Carson, wake up. Carson. Hey, Carson."

Eventually the dead will rise, and out will come our ever-comical merch man.

RUNNIN' OUR WAY

"The life I love is makin' music with my friends."

The Willie Nelson classic "On the Road Again" is a song we use to sum up 2013 on the series of videos we call ScotTV. We've made a dozen of the videos highlighting some of the memories of the band on the road, including the story mentioned earlier where Dylan does his march-jump-kick routine. So we take all the highlights and show them while Jeff and I do a cover of the song. It really does fit, not just for this year but for all the years we've been touring.

I'm not a roller-coaster guy, and Scotty was aware of that; however, through his gift for words, he convinced me to join him that dark night at Six Flags on a "tiny roller coaster." I had no idea what was in store until I was strapped in next to him and heard an announcer say, "Welcome to El Toro—the world's second-fastest wooden roller coaster." As we pulled away, I looked over at Scotty and saw him chuckling.

JUSTIN WARD, GUITARIST

It's fun to do the videos, and it's also a bit ironic since I've already had my fair share of time on the screen. I'm used to having a camera filming me. What I love is that I really can call these guys brothers. I spent a couple years in college, but I soon realize *these guys* are kind of like my classmates. Touring, performing, making albums, and being in this business—that's my education.

I'll say it again—I'm fortunate to have these guys around me. "Like a band of gypsies we go down the highway." Thankfully, we manage to laugh a lot along the way.

"YOU DROPPED A BOMB ON ME"

Everyone knows I love traditional country music, but that doesn't mean I haven't listened to other genres.

Here's a little-known fact: I do love some R&B/Funk. I had the opportunity to meet a legend in this genre by the name of Charlie Wilson. That's right, Charlie Wilson of The Gap Band, who sang the classic "You Dropped a Bomb on Me."

In 2007, I was thirteen and was heading to West Lake Middle School with wonderful Bernetta Smith driving car pool. She was so wonderful because she had us listening to Foxy 107 on the way to West Lake. Until then, I'd pretty much been a 94.7 WQDR country radio guy.

One morning as we were cruising down Old Stage Road, I heard the song.

"My name is Charlie, last name Wilson . . ."

This sounds great.

It's smooth and classic. And his voice . . .

"I was wondering . . . if I could take you out . . ."

This guy's legit.

I would learn his name. This was how I discovered Uncle Charlie Wilson.

Fast-forward to 2011 when I was on *Idol*. We were down to the Top 7, and I'm in Santa Monica at one of Interscope's recording studios, meeting with producer Rodney Jerkins. We're all throwing out song ideas for this week's show. This was always a tall task because everyone has an opinion.

"Hey, y'all. How 'bout a little Uncle Charlie?" I asked them.

They looked at me with puzzled expressions. I then proceeded to shock them with my smoothest "my name is Scotty, last name McCreery." I had them rolling. They loved it! Rodney kept saying, "Uncle Charlie's gonna love this!"

What they said next, however, was something to this effect: "Don't you think you'll confuse your fans?"

Well, they had a good point. Up to then, I had been "in my lane"—as Randy Jackson said, "keeping it country."

Fast-forward to 2015. I had covered Uncle

Charlie a time or two at different events. We had retweeted and followed one another on Twitter too. I see Uncle Charlie is coming to Raleigh's PNC Arena, so I reach out, letting him know I bought tickets and will be taking a group to see him.

Holy smokes—it's just like going to the Wynn in Vegas to see Garth. I get to the arena, and Charlie sends one of his guys to find me. He tells me Charlie wants me to join him onstage.

What?

I'm about to have a stroke. I didn't prepare for this! The man is a legend, and I'm about to join him onstage, wearing jeans and a Wolfpack pullover? But if Charlie wants me onstage with him, I'm there.

Now Charlie's crowd is a little different from a typical Scotty crowd. I had to win them over. But when I start singing, the reaction is crazy. Truly a moment I will never forget.

After the show, he invites me and my friends to his dressing room for pictures, some eats, and a chance to meet his lovely wife, Mahin. He's a class act all the way.

He releases a great book in 2015, and he sends me an autographed copy.

Thanks, Uncle Charlie. And thanks, Ms. Bernetta, for tuning in to Foxy 107.

Maybe one day I can be an Uncle Scotty to someone.

HEADLINING

It's Memorial Day 2014. I head toward Brad Paisley's bus and knock on the door. Soon I'm chatting with him on his bus.

"Hey, man, I just thought I'd stop by and say thanks," I tell him. "I mean—you know, I thought it'd take longer before this moment would come. I've only been doing this for a couple of years, but thanks. I appreciate you opening up for me, Brad. I mean it."

We both laugh but it's true. *Brad Paisley is opening up for me.*

Of course, it takes an executive order to make this happen.

We're playing a festival with Brad and others when suddenly we learn a few days beforehand that we'll be headlining it. None of us know why, not even Brad's dad or tour manager. All we know is that Paisley and his band will be playing at 2:00 p.m. In the middle of the day when the light is still nice and bright.

His band is thrilled. They haven't played during the day in a long time. And of course, we're ecstatic. A few of the other acts aren't so thrilled once they learn we're taking Brad's place. It's another nice gesture from a gentleman.

Soon enough, we discover why the singer had to leave the show early. It turns out Brad makes a surprise stop to an airfield in Afghanistan to play for three thousand troops. He just so happens to fly over there with President Obama on Air Force One.

How cool is *that?*

I'm sure Paisley was sitting on that plane wondering the same thing I'm wondering while performing that night in front of thousands.

How'd I get here in the first place?

There are lots and lots of miles covered before you find yourself in that moment. But I know one thing: It's not about the destination; it's about the journey.

And it's also about those who take the journey with you.

Chapter Thirteen

Blessed to
Be a Blessing

There's a pause and short silence near the end of my song "The Dash." In a way, this can resemble our lives at times. It's loud and moving along, and then suddenly something happens that takes our breath away, that puts life on hold. An illness or a death or a personal letdown or a national tragedy. Yet like the steady beat and the continuing melody of that song, our lives go on. They have to. And as they do, music is there to help and sometimes to even heal.

One of the most humbling and fulfilling parts of performing music is to know it can do both of those things. God can give hope through songs and melodies. He gave those two things to us, so why shouldn't music be able to heal and inspire us when life becomes tough?

I can think of some memorable moments I've had when it comes to meeting people who have inspired *me,* even while I was there hoping to do the same for them.

A LITTLE HAPPINESS

I've sung on lots of special stages, and this one is no exception. Jeff, Dylan, and I are on the Butterfly Stage, performing acoustic songs for a special group of people today. I sing "I Love You This Big" and see several guests singing along. It's good to see their smiles.

We're at the Monroe Carell Jr. Children's Hospital at Vanderbilt University participating in the Opry's "Cause for Applause." The Grand Ole Opry is celebrating nine decades of country music, and they've been bringing artists and fans together in support of different charities and causes. I'll sing some songs and give the kids a special present—a Grand Ole Opry train whistle from the Opry's vintage toy collection.

More than singing and giving, we're here to share some greetings and hopefully some joy.

This hospital really is an amazing place. The second floor, called Main Street, has a gift shop, a food court, and a chapel at the end of the hall. The ceilings are colorful, and the walls look like they've been transported out of some kid's four-color book. There are fish tanks, trains, playgrounds, activity centers, and a movie theater.

They want kids to not only feel special but also to somehow forget they're in a hospital. That might be impossible, but at least Vanderbilt is trying as hard as possible to make something about this experience *fun*.

On that same floor is a room for families called the Family Resource Center. Here the hospital helps families learn about their child's illness or disability. A customized patient package is created for families so they get more info. There's also a full library for checking out books and resources, along with a whole section for kids.

The hospital has places where families can stay that include a kitchen and laundry room.

After our small set, I meet the kids and parents. One woman holding a picture of her newborn child in intensive care asks to take a picture with me. I put my arm around a ten-year-old boy sitting in a wheelchair as someone takes our picture. I sign an autograph and say hi to another woman holding her newborn.

Tiny little lives—children of all ages—all here for various reasons. They applaud us for visiting them, but I can only think of what *they're* going through. And what the doctors and nurses do on a daily basis. Calling them heroes may sound trite, but it's true.

I'm just a singer. But thank God for music, because it never ceases to create a little happiness in places that certainly need it.

ANY SORT OF JOY AND LIGHT

It's a small community just like Garner. I get this town and the people living here. I just don't get what occurred here.

It seems to always happen in a small town just like this. That's 'cause there are so many of them in our country. Towns full of folks living their lives and trying to do good and raising families and making a living when their entire world blows up in the worst way possible.

That's why I'm here. 'Cause if there's just one ounce of hope or inspiration I can share with these folks, then I'm happy to do it.

It's two days before the first anniversary of the Sandy Hook Elementary School shootings in Newtown, Connecticut. I sure remember where I was in 2012 when I heard news of the tragedy. A senseless thing like a school shooting has become an all-too-familiar topic on the news, but this event was different. This shooting happened at an elementary school.

Eight boys and twelve girls were gunned down that day, all of them between the ages of six and seven. Another six adults working at Sandy Hook also lost their lives.

It's difficult to fathom how this could happen in such a charming little community. When I get a chance to meet with the people, I see how strong they are. I hope and pray I can do what they're doing—spreading the word. Telling kids to cling to hope. And that's why they've invited me here. To bring some of that.

To say it's humbling doesn't even begin to match how I'm feeling.

All I want to do is to show kids who've lived through a nightmare that sometimes dreams can come true. I have seen that music is one of those things that can get people through tough times. So when community leaders asked if I could come, I didn't hesitate. There was no question.

If I can do anything positive and bring any joy and light to this place, I'm doing it.

Dr. Michael Baroody is one of the reasons I'm here. As the father of two young children, he started the 12.14 Foundation after the horrific event in Newtown. His desire was to help hurting children and the entire community. He set out to contact the very best people to help him achieve the goal of building a world-class performing arts center to memorialize those who lost their lives and to use the arts as a vessel to heal. Dr. Baroody wants to make sure this tragedy doesn't prevent any of them from reaching their full potential.

Dr. Baroody knew there was a way to combat the grief gripping their children and the entire community. He believes the performing arts are able to help kids express themselves in different ways, and that this foundation can help them begin to cope with the senseless tragedy.

> We initially wanted Scotty to perform a benefit concert, but after a few conversations, we asked him to become a goodwill ambassador for the 12.14 Foundation. Scotty is the type of role model we want for the kids in Newtown. He is humble, hard-working, accomplished at a young age, and has overcome many obstacles to achieve success. On a personal level, I will always be indebted to Scotty for being one of the first to join us and truly believe in our mission.
>
> DR. MICHAEL BAROODY

Since he didn't know many people in the arts world, he began to Google names and reach out to all sorts of people—musicians, choreographers, designers, and actors. That's how I ended up being contacted and asked to become a goodwill ambassador for their foundation. Having grown up in the performing arts, I obviously know and love this world. To try to inspire some kids in that arena—it's a pretty awesome opportunity.

I realize something now more than ever: Having a number one record might be a nice goal, but impacting people in a positive and powerful way is my main goal. The 12.14 Foundation is doing this through music and the performing arts, so I can't think of a better fit.

The radio and television interviews help spread the word. The concert raises some money. But being here and talking and singing—this isn't about me. It's not about Scotty McCreery adding one more notch on his charity belt.

"It's not about me; it's about what these folks can do here," I tell a reporter.

There's no way it can be about me. Not after hearing the stories and seeing the eyes of the men, women, and children who've been affected.

"This is something that will never go away," I say in my television interview. "This will always be a part of what happened here. But this town is not defined by this. There are great people here, and it's a great community. We're really trying to take a tragedy and bring some hope through this."

When I'm able to perform in front of the community and raise money for the foundation, I share my belief about the power of music.

"I've always believed music is a lot more than just chords and lyrics. It can be very healing and can touch the lives of many people."

I've been given so much and have had the opportunity to see my dreams come true through music. To be involved in something like this and combat some of the darkness in this world is the reason God allowed me to get to this point.

Hopefully, one day, when the performing arts

center is up and running, I'll return to perform. I can't wait to see the hope that blossomed through the seeds planted by people like Dr. Baroody.

A TRUE INSPIRATION

I visit Dylan Price for the first time the November after winning *American Idol* the previous May. Our families are connected through church, so when I hear about his battle with cancer and learn he's a big fan of mine, I schedule a visit with him and his family at UNC Children's Hospital in Chapel Hill, North Carolina.

I learn that Dylan's folks were going to give him guitar lessons for Christmas but then found out he was sick. He actually begins lessons after coming to the hospital. They tell me the music therapy program there has taught him everything he knows.

He plays a tune for me, and I'm impressed.

"You're good," I say. "You got rhythm."

Dylan tells me about rooting for me during *Idol* and how glad he was when I won. We share a few moments and memories, and I'm glad to have connected with the young kid. Dylan is fourteen, three years younger than me. As I spend time with him, I see so much of myself when I was his age. He's active in church, loves his school, and loves the guitar.

Why am I not the sick one? Why him? Why not me?

It turns out Dylan is quite a fighter. He survives leukemia and has a bone marrow transplant. After the transplant, he has two heart attacks but still manages to live. Dylan begins to live life like a normal teen.

Dylan inspires all those around him through his attitude and the way he decides to seize life.

There's always the risk of a heart attack after a transplant. But he doesn't live his life in fear. He does the opposite—Dylan inspires hope.

Scotty appeared at a show in Katy, Texas, in November, and I took both my daughter and granddaughter. Afterward, we had a private meet and greet on Scotty's tour bus. We took pictures, chatted, and had Scotty sign the guitar I'd purchased earlier. As we were leaving, my granddaughter Catherine asked for a private moment with Scotty. When she rejoined us, she told me she had shown Scotty a photo he'd taken with her husband, Adam, a couple years before. She wanted to tell Scotty how much "The Dash" meant to her after Adam's death a year ago in a tragic auto accident. She said Scotty was so sweet. He gave her a big hug and thanked her. This is the Scotty we love.

L. MATJEKA AND C. OXFORD,
McCREERIANS FROM TEXAS

He's a teenager who suddenly has his whole life changed. Dylan will say cancer is an awakening. He decides to live life to the fullest and do the things he's always wanted to do. Simple things like going to high school and getting a driver's license and even falling in love.

Dylan can't do anything about the cancer in his body. But he can make sure it doesn't eat away at his soul.

The valiant and courageous young man passes away after a third heart attack. His last post on Facebook shares his motto in life:

"The brave might not live forever, but the cautious never live at all."

Our paths crossed simply because Dylan was a fan of the show and my singing. I was able to cheer him up a bit by visiting the hospital that day. What he did for me, however, was to inspire me by reminding me how blessed I am. He reminded me how precious life is. And how we have to keep going, despite what life might bring.

One of my songs, "The Dash," talks about how you're supposed to live between your first breath and your last. Life shouldn't be measured by the number of years but rather by the journey you've taken.

This song and these lyrics remind me of someone like Dylan, a brave young guy making the most of his short life.

CONNECTIONS

I've heard many stories from my fans who connected with my music during a tough time in their lives. Because of *American Idol*, there were relationships created and bonds built out of support for me.

I heard stories about chats at the water cooler and excited kids talking on school buses. A hospital nurse who worked the evening shift told me several patients insisted she watch *Idol* with them. One woman told me she was only given a warning ticket when the police officer who pulled her over saw she was wearing a "Vote for Scotty" button.

Craziness, right?

My sis told me her apartment at UNC-Charlotte was full of college students with laptops open and phones ready to vote when *Idol* aired.

My fan club started the moment people began to see me performing on *Idol*. There were forums, blogs, and groups of different ages and backgrounds from all over the country (and even overseas, wherever *Idol* was seen) who rallied around me. I've heard some of these die-hard fans have not only gotten to meet one another in person but have become close friends. It's great knowing some of those connections have resulted in deep friendships and helped others who are dealing with depression or loss.

Josh Turner once said, "To think that my heart and my words and my music saved somebody's life—it takes a while to just sink in with me. But it proves to me that music is powerful."

I completely agree. I hear stories and comments from fans and feel many things. I feel grateful, humbled, and inspired to keep singing and performing. I want to make music that gives people hope.

It's just amazing I'm able to bring joy and happiness through my singing. I love the surprise element too. My former elementary teacher, Beth Palmieri, asked me to surprise her chorus class in May 2015. It sounded too fun to say no. Her class at Timber Drive Elementary, my old stomping grounds, was learning my first single, "I Love You This Big," for their end-of-year performance. Ms. Palmieri asked if I would be in town and if I could surprise the kids and join them while they were singing. And just as we planned, while they were warming up, I slipped in the side door of the auditorium. Amid the gasps and surprised looks, I jumped onto the stage, and we made a moment. The curtain was pulled down after the warm-up time, and we prepared ourselves to give the Garner parents a surprise as well.

Good times. What continued to make the evening great was the Make-A-Wish Foundation had arranged for me to meet a local heart transplant recipient, eighteen-year-old Courtney Moss.

311

My wife had recently died of cancer, and I was really missing her. I was crying on the sofa, with the TV playing softly for some noise in a quiet house. Suddenly, this marvel-ous voice grabbed me, like a gift from God jarring me into reality. It was Scotty singing "Long Black Train" on *American Idol*. I quickly turned up the sound, and a sense of peace flooded into my soul that I hadn't felt in a long time. Over the years, Scotty's music and soothing baritone voice have truly been gifts from God that continue to fill my life with happiness.

MOE DEPIERO,
McCREERIAN FROM WINNIPEG, ANITOBA

Courtney would actually be at the *Idol* finale in a couple weeks, and I was doing the send-off.

Hospital visits, bringing a smile to a hurting community, surprising some hometown chorus students—it doesn't get any better. I love these opportunities to lift up others. It's a remarkable thing to be told you've helped someone by doing the very thing you love to do.

I'm not a doctor, a nurse, a police officer, a soldier, or even a parent. I'm a singer with a low voice who seems to make people smile. And that's a cool thing.

As long as people keep smiling, I'll keep singing.

Chapter Fourteen

Special Places and Lots of Faces

It's June 2015, and I'm at the Grand Ole Opry. Never a place to forget, and never a place to take for granted if you're standing on its historic stage. While some in the audience know the song I'm about to sing, I'm here to sing for those who have only heard contemporary country hits. The ones who have never been personally greeted by a deep voice saying six simple words: "Hello darlin', nice to see you."

The story goes that Conway Twitty originally sang the opening lines of his signature song, but they just didn't work. The producer suggested he speak them instead. And just like that, a classic was born.

Now here's the thing with classics. Songs that unmistakably belong to the artists who sing them are dangerous songs to cover.

Take "That's All Right" by Elvis Presley. Come on. Listen to the song. The voice is like a tightened fist about to strike. High, pure, and just electric. Not the easiest song to try to make your own.

Or take "The Grand Tour" by George Jones. Its

fragile, aged, and timeless tone is impossible to duplicate.

Then there's "The Dance" by Garth. Do I even need to say the last name? This loaded voice full of a thousand stories will unfold and probably break your heart.

These songs are country staples, so it can sometimes be disastrous when trying to cover them. They are so identified with their original singer in the hearts and minds of music fans. Yet they're all songs I've been fortunate enough to sing in front of folks on the very stage I'm standing on tonight. The grand but intimate, ole but young at heart, one and only Opry.

Hopefully, I might have introduced a few folks to some classics they just have to check out. Like tonight's song.

I imagine someone asking, "Who sings this? Conway *who?*"

I know, I know. Could anybody even ask that question? There's no way someone hasn't heard of Conway Twitty, right?

Here's something a lot of people might not know about Conway. Something that reminds me a lot of myself. He started a band named the Phillips County Ramblers when he was only ten years old. His love of country music was equaled only by his love of baseball. In fact, he was drafted to play baseball after high school by the Philadelphia Phillies. And then someone else drafted him—Uncle Sam. And that dashed his dream of playing baseball.

Conway once said he never imagined competing against the same folks he'd hear singing on Grand Ole Opry broadcasts when he was younger. And just like Conway, I never pictured myself singing one of his songs while standing in front of this crowd.

Maybe there's someone who never pictured himself falling in love with a classic song they've never heard. So just in case, I'll keep the covers coming.

Conway, Elvis, George, and Garth are those one-of-a-kind souls with very large shadows. I'm happy to stand in those shadows and allow the gracious spotlight of the Grand Ole Opry to shine on me for a moment to remind others about them.

THE GRAND OLE OPRY

On June 13, 2011, I made my debut at the Opry, along with my *Idol* comrade Lauren Alaina. A little more than two weeks earlier, the finale of *American Idol* had been watched by almost thirty million people. But performing in front of the four-thousand-plus Opry crowd feels just as exciting. I couldn't keep myself from grinning when I came onstage to sing.

"It's such an honor to be here tonight," I told everybody watching.

Earlier in the week, Carrie Underwood introduced Lauren and me at the Opry and talked about our upcoming debut. The night of our official debut was a special date since it was six years ago to the day when Carrie Underwood made her first appearance.

Since my Opry debut, I've stepped onto that six-foot oak circle of center stage more than fifteen times. The Opry started out as the "WSM Barn Dance," a one-hour radio show broadcast live from the studio of WSM-AM radio station in Nashville in 1925. Its popularity grew so much that crowds began to come to watch the broadcasts. As the crowds got bigger, WSM moved the show to several different venues in Nashville before ultimately taking up residence at the now world-famous Ryman Auditorium in 1943. The show remained at the Ryman until 1974, when it moved into the brand-new Grand Ole Opry House.

My idol, Elvis, performed at the Ryman one time, and one time only. This was the infamous "go back to driving trucks" incident I mentioned earlier, where they didn't quite get his style of music. He vowed to never come back, and he didn't.

Here's an interesting side note about an industry professional, Beverly Keel, a journalist and public relations specialist, who was with me when I made my Opry debut. At that time, Beverly was the vice president for artist relations at my label.

Beverly told me many years earlier that her father, Pinckney Keel, also a journalist, gave Elvis the nickname "Elvis the Pelvis" when Pinckney was a reporter at the Clarion-Ledger in Jackson, Mississippi. The name stuck, and the rest is history. I was thinking, *Wow, the same family that did some press for Elvis is now doing some press for me.*

CMA MUSIC FESTIVAL

The following morning is sticky-hot in Nashville. We're having our fan club party at a place called Rocketown. I'll do a small show today, along with a Q&A. There will be lunch, door prizes, and a meet and greet where fans can get their picture with me. Oh, and souvenir Scotty McCreery sunglasses.

There was a day when I would have thought Scotty sunglasses was someone's idea of a joke. But hey, I gotta admit—they're pretty cool. Especially the red ones.

I arrive at Rocketown wearing shorts and a T-shirt before I change clothes in my bus. Regular Scotty wears a baseball cap backward and a faded Wolfpack T-shirt. Singer Scotty wears boots and jeans and a custom-fit, button-down shirt. One of the faithful McCreerians, Wanda Soares from Indiana, knows both Scottys well as she approaches us with her tray of goodies. Wanda has been to almost thirty of my shows. She's also in my fan club, where she scores meet-and-greet passes pretty often. After talking with her for a few minutes, we head to the tour bus where I'll get ready.

"I gotta try this stuff out," tour manager Mike says as he grabs one of Wanda's no-bake cookies.

It's funny, 'cause Mike says this a lot. And he's always sampling the goods, whether it's no-bake cookies, brownies, or banana nut bread. My fans sure do love me, and my tour manager sure does love them.

I know my unique connection with my fans comes from the *Idol* days, from the families and grandparents and young kids voting for me week

---

In the eleven years I've worked at Fan Clubhouse, I've never seen a fan club as diverse as Scotty's. The McCreerians range from small children three or four years old to fans in their nineties. It's great to see Scotty's music touch so many people, all at different stages of life. It's a true testament to the value of his music and his character. The fan club continues to grow as new people discover Scotty's music every day!

RACHEL SLATE,
FAN CLUBHOUSE, NASHVILLE

---

after week. People have described my fan base as ages four to ninety-four. I've seen it firsthand. I can't tell you how many people I run across who say, "We voted for you every week!" Most don't say this in a way that makes it sound like I owe them, and I never take it like that. But it didn't take years, like it has for many artists, for fans to fall in love with me. For me, it was almost over-night.

I don't use the "fall in love with me" phrase in some kind of cocky way. I say it from having lived with it for five years. There's an incredible amount of passion and devotion from my fans.

It humbles me.

It also drives me.

People have remarked about how polite I am. Or about how mature I am for my age. About my quiet confidence. About the comfort I feel in being a country singer.

When I sang "You Got a Friend" on *Idol*, a lot of my fans felt like I was singing it to them. And in a way, I *was* performing it to them.

I'm not unique in being a Southern gentleman. I'm not the only one who carries my faith, not like a coat you wear some of the time, but more like a ring you always keep on. I'm not the only one who loves country or the only person confident in their own skin. There are so many others who are just like me, waiting for their big break. But first they might be waiting for that extra bit of encourage-ment from a friend or family member to set them on their way.

My love of songs and the gift to sing them—those two things have intersected, along with many other things, to create the man I am. Many, many people have watched the boy who very quickly became that young man. There are so many fans and supporters I'm grateful for.

I can't personally say hi to or even have a way to know all the people who have enjoyed my singing and my journey. But I do my best to connect with them in some way. It might be during a fan club meet and greet, where I have only a minute to simply say hello. It might be the hour or two I'm on a stage in front of them. That's when I'm the professional musician giving it my all and trying my best to entertain. Even when I'm in the studio working on new songs and recording them, it's for the fans.

The song choices are made with my fans in mind.

I may not be able to know all my fans, but through my music I am forming a relationship with them and doing my best to carry them with me wherever I go.

THE FANS

"Hi, Scotty. My name is Susan, and I'm from Greensburg, Pennsylvania."

"Hey, hey," I say into the mic.

"It's my daughter's twenty-first birthday, and I was wondering if you could sing Happy Birthday to her?"

I smile. "Give me a key, boys."

The crowd in Rocketown gives me a collective "Awww," while Dylan strums a few chords on his guitar.

"Happy birthday to you. Happy birthday to you. Happy birthday, dear . . . stop—what's her name again?"

"Annie," the woman says.

"Amy?"

"Annie."

"ANN-EEE," I say/sing. "Happy birthday to you."

It's Q&A time at our Scotty fan club party. Or "sing a song to your daughter" time. I love events like this. It's great because it really gives me a picture of my fans, the McCreerians. We like to say they range from toddlers in their strollers to grandmas with their walkers. A look into the crowd confirms this.

The questions run the gamut from the basic to the deep. From favorite ice cream flavors to who influenced me the most as a musician growing up to even asking about my girlfriend.

"I'd like to ask how you asked Gabby out."

"Guh-Bee," I pronounce.

She's Cajun, so her name is a little different.

I share the story about the video for "The Trouble with Girls" and how I ended up switching Kyle Wiggins with Gabi. As I share the story, I hear lots of laughter and a few "awwws." It wouldn't have been easy for me to share this in front of all these people five years ago, but I've grown very comfortable sitting on stage and speaking into a mic. Especially when I'm talking to my fans.

A typical exchange shows how comfortable they talk with—and tease—me.

"You know what I named my boat? Sea You Tonite. S-E-A."

A woman in the audience calls out, "Ain't you clever," and everybody laughs.

"Yeah, I was also thinking of Reelin' It, but . . ." I say, trailing off. "Someone stop me up here."

I even have a girl come up and playfully taunt me about how her New York Giants have beaten my New England Patriots in the Super Bowl twice. Man, these fans aren't holding back. But that's why I love these people.

"My name is Amber, and I'm from Bloomington, Indiana. And I'd like to know who you like better—Elvis Presley or Johnny Cash."

Lots of oohs and aahs.

"Really?" I ask in complete disbelief.

There's no question.

"I mean, Elvis was by far my guy," I say. "But I'm not hating on Cash—I mean, the 'man in black.' And lemme tell ya, I've met Merle Haggard and seen him live. He ranks right up there. But I gotta choose Elvis. I've loved him since I was a kid."

When the questions are done, I'm able to perform some songs and even share a couple of very brief clips from some songs on the new album. I tell everyone my label won't like me doing this, so I ask that nobody record them. The response is great, even though I only play twenty or thirty seconds of each song.

The performance ends with a nice little surprise. Especially for our *Idol* fans. My partner in crime shows up. I had spontaneously texted her an hour earlier. Lauren Alaina had dropped by the Opry last night and stopped by my dressing room to say hi and chat for a while. It felt like old times—Lauren smiling, laughing, and talking, and me just nodding. She talked about her upcoming songs and what she was doing with her music. We also shared a few stories about what was happening with some of our *Idol* family.

Lauren receives a warm welcome from the crowd. We end up covering the Randy Travis tune "I Told You So," a song we performed on *Idol* in the Top 11 show.

Lauren's voice is still absolute dynamite. Her delivery of the chorus receives applause. Such strength. The girl's only gotten better in the four-plus years since we sang that song. She hasn't changed, though. Lauren still giggles and shakes her head with that smile America loved.

Man . . . four years.

It feels like *Idol* was just a few weeks ago. Then again, it also feels like a decade ago.

"Lauren Alaina, everybody!" I say after we finish the song and hug one another.

As she leaves the stage, I just shake my head.

"Unbelievable," I say into the mic.

They say to surround yourself with talented people. Well, I've sure been surrounded by amazing talent ever since Hollywood Week.

SINGING IN THE PARK

It's stifling hot, the kind of heat that's just not good for wearing jeans and boots. But Superman has his cape, and I've got mine. The crowd doesn't seem to mind the hot sun because they're listening to music surrounded by friends chillin', drinkin', and laughin'. They've already heard several acts on the Riverfront stage. My job is to keep the good vibes flowing and to create an impression.

It's fun to be able to perform "Whiplash" from the upcoming album. Few people have heard it, and those who have only know it from the few times I've performed it live. Still, it's a rockin', get-the-people-movin' sort of tune. It's a cowrite I did recently with David Lee Murphy, a great

> I've been an avid Scotty fan since *American Idol*. Love his fantastic vocals and his charming, down-to-earth personality. I've attended numerous concerts in six states and been lucky enough to meet him. Such a sweetie—and his concerts are a blast. His energy is so contagious that I'm on my feet the entire time dancing and singing along. He's truly one of a kind!
>
> DAWN PERRETTI JOBLON,
> McCREERIAN FROM
> WESTFIELD, NEW JERSEY

writer who's also had massive hits of his own.

It doesn't matter if it's a hundred people or several thousand in the audience. I do my best to connect, get people interested, and create energy. I share bits between the songs about the *Idol* experience, about CMA Music Festival, and about my upcoming album.

Lots of people from my Nashville team are here. All watching. Seeing how Scotty's doing. Seeing how the crowd is looking, how we're sounding, and what the overall buzz is like.

When you have the spotlight centered on you for so long, day and night, whether live or taped for an audience, you grow used to it. Some might grow numb, but that's not how I'm feeling. I'm excited and grateful. I still have shows to do. It's a life I dearly love, a life that's a gift. But I still have to get up, go out there, and give it all I can. It's my moment to work, so I'm working as hard as I can to get the crowd on its feet, to make my fans forget about their problems.

By the faces and the heads and bodies moving, singing, and smiling, I can see I'm doing my job.

Chapter Fifteen

Business, Balance, and Blessings

I get the emergency warning to get indoors and protect myself. While I appreciate my cell phone trying to save my life, all my bandmates already got the text. They just happened to get their life-and-death messages several minutes ago.

The upcoming show in Tinley Park, Illinois, might be the first I'll ever have to cancel. The poor fans are still outside the gates of the First Midwest Bank Amphitheatre, standing in the rain and wondering if they'll be let in. We sit in the dressing room, all of us in a circle, talking about the September storm and playing one of the games we might typically play before a concert.

The game consists of the following: Someone starts with the name of a movie, and then the next guy has to say the name of an actor in that movie. The next person has to name a different movie that the actor was in, and it just keeps going from there.

Then the chatter turns to work. Since we'll be playing at the Opry in a few nights, we begin to throw out song ideas. Earlier this year when I performed at the Ryman, I sang "Hello Darlin'."

It was quite the hit, with more than three million views on YouTube in less than a year of its posting.

Mike suggests we sing some crowd favorites, while Dylan throws a few curveballs with some songs I've never heard. We go back and forth, with Mike and Jeff on their iPhones listening to music we might want to perform. I'm twirling my phone around while we wait for word on whether we'll perform. We continue playing our game and tossing around song choices.

It's how we live on the road, mixing work and play. This is our profession. Music is our livelihood. I might get the chance to be the one the crowd cheers for the most, the guy front and center singing and selling T-shirts with his face on it. I'm also the CEO of Team Scotty. And that means I have responsibilities, including making sure these guys around me are being taken care of.

The fact is, I have about a dozen guys on my payroll. Guys I love and want to take care of. These guys have families and depend on me to provide for them. Most of my band and crew are married with kids. Lots of kids. Four of my guys have either three or four kids.

I sure hope we can get out there and perform tonight. A cancellation isn't going to be good for any of us.

ALL IN A DAY'S WORK

The show in Tinley Park finally happens. We get to do our full setlist, but unfortunately, the opening act—a fabulous singer named Ashley Monroe—doesn't get to perform. It's especially unfortunate for the fans who have never seen her perform. Live shows are an important way for new artists to build their fan base. We finish the show and stay up until 2:00 a.m. before heading to our bunks as the bus pulls out for Cincinnati.

Here's the agenda for the show in Cincy, our operating orders that Mike and his team put together.

SATURDAY, SEPTEMBER 19, 2015

SCOTTY MCCREERY RASCAL FLATTS TOUR, <u>CINCINNATI, OHIO</u>

- Breakfast: 7:00 a.m.–10:00 a.m.
- Load In: 11:00 a.m.
- Lunch: 12:00 p.m.–3:00 p.m.
- Push Gear/Setup: 1:00 p.m.
- Scotty Sound Check: 3:30 p.m.–4:15 p.m.
- Scotty Group Appearance: 4:30 p.m.
- Dinner: 5:00 p.m.–8:00 p.m.
- Doors: 6:00 p.m.
- Scotty W/ PR: 6:15 p.m.

- Scotty VIP M&G: 6:35 p.m.–6:50 p.m.
- Scotty Fan Club M&G: 6:50 p.m.–7:20 p.m.
- Ashley Monroe Showtime: 7:30 p.m.– 7:50 p.m.
- Stage Reset: 7:50 p.m.–8:05 p.m.
- Scotty Showtime: 8:05 p.m.–8:45 p.m.
- Scotty Load Out: 8:45 p.m.–10:00 p.m.
- Stage Reset: 8:45 p.m.–9:00 p.m.
- Rascal Flatts: 9:20 p.m.–11:00 p.m.
- Driver Call: 12:00 a.m.
- Everyone Drive to Van Wert, OH (159 miles/3 hours): 1:00 a.m.–4:00 a.m.

We have nine hours of the day allotted for eating. You can see where our priorities are. But seriously, this allows for some flexibility during the day. There's a lot of business to attend to; it's just not necessarily tour business. The nights are intense, and we have to be 100 percent ready, so we strive to do everything we can to be prepared.

I enjoy touring and always have, but I don't like being *this* busy. Two weeks on the road is usually my max, but during the past two months, I think I've had five days off. I need those days off to recharge my batteries. Tonight is a Rascal Flatts tour, so we'll have forty minutes to perform before they come on. For the shows we headline, we'll perform for an hour and a half.

There are fun and exciting parts to this life. There's also the not-so-glamorous side—like living out of a bus, waking up in the parking lots of concert venues, and getting used to showering in dressing rooms—with a fifty-fifty chance there's hot water.

One of the worst things can be getting sick far from home. I'm a pretty healthy guy—knock on wood. To date, I've never had to cancel a show because of sickness. After a show out west, however, I crawled into my bunk with chills and a fever. I had felt terrible just before going onstage and knew something was wrong. My roommate Colin at NC State had the flu, and I had a sneaking suspicion I was coming down with it, even though I had gotten my flu shot. I texted my doc in North Carolina at 1:00 a.m. and told him my symptoms, to which he promptly responded, "Congrats, Scotty, you have a full-fledged case of the flu. Where should I call in the Tamiflu?" I said, "Um, know any pharmacies in Nebraska?"

JUST GETTING STARTED

The business of being a musician is a 24/7 preoccupation. I go to sleep thinking about it and wake up with it still on my mind. And for good reason.

Some in the industry say there's a five-year life span for an artist. And by my count, I'm approaching that number. Five years is coming up very soon.

Winning *Idol* starts an artist at the top, and then we must figure out how to make this music thing grow and last. For a country artist like me, I may end up doing 150 to 200 performances a year. That includes big concerts and smaller promotional events. My goal is to become established enough to both sell out shows and dictate how many shows I'd like to do, as well as build other revenue streams.

The year 2015 has been busy, and not just because I'm touring. I'm making a new album and working on several other projects—this book, for example. The year 2016 looks to be just as crazy. It's *American Idol*'s farewell season.

What Scotty McCreery really has is presence. He's kind of like a young Marlon Brando walking onto a stage. You just know something good is coming. The stage is his . . . If I was guessing, and I am, I'd say that McCreery is going to carve a new niche in country music, between the revered olden days and the frantic pop-country that we have now. And that niche is going to be a wonderful treat for everyone who listens to country music.

DAVE BEGEL,
ONMILWAUKEE.COM, JUNE 27, 2014

Ashley is getting married. Gabi is graduating from nursing school. Just two months into 2016, and I've already performed from Canada to Mexico—with lots of places in between. My new album is being released. There are lots of things happening.

But that five-year life span? I'm fighting to change that and to prove the trends wrong. And I believe things are both looking up and heading up. Of course, I know there will be challenges along the way.

One thing folks don't realize is there's never been a teenage guy to blow up in country music. Teenage ladies have been able to pull it off (Taylor Swift, LeAnn Rimes, Tanya Tucker), but to date, very few teenage males have experienced lasting success in country music. Most country males don't seem to make it big until their late twenties or early thirties. Who knows why. Maybe some think they need to pay their dues first. Some even think winning *American Idol* is the easy way to success.

Trust me—there's nothing easy about singing live in front of twenty or thirty million viewers week after week. Especially if you're seventeen with no professional experience.

But just like I said at the *Idol* homecoming in Garner, I'm gonna keep workin' my tail off, singing my songs, showing up at those fan club parties and meet and greets, and writing and recording with the best in the business. Hey, I'm only twenty-two. I'm very fortunate, humbled, and blessed to already have three number one album debuts, three platinum singles, millions of YouTube views, and several industry awards, including the Academy of Country Music (ACM) award for Best New Artist. I've also got a dedicated fan base and an amazing band and crew I love.

I'm just getting started.

THE NEW ALBUM

It's just one word. One single word. And I swear I can't get it right.

"Let's try it again," Frank says as he sits behind a massive control panel and jots notes on a sheet of paper.

"Any other girl . . ." I start to sing in the microphone for ten seconds. Then stop again. I look through the glass window at my producer.

There's one word, and something's not working.

"I like that concept," Frank tells me. "Let's get a couple takes."

I'm in a familiar place I've seen a lot of lately—Frank Rogers's home studio in Nashville. I'm here with Frank and his sound engineer, Richard Barrow. Both are well-known and respected in the business. It's the second album I've worked on with Frank. He produced *See You Tonight*. I loved both the results and the experience.

Growing up as a kid, I was a big fan of Frank's work, even if I didn't know it. Once I got in the business, I really wanted to work with him. His first claim to fame was working with Brad Paisley. I often tell people that one of my favorite songs is "I'm Gonna Miss Her" by Brad Paisley. Frank cowrote the song. He's worked with numerous other artists like Trace Adkins, Josh Turner, and Darius Rucker.

Frank really has the sound and vibe I'm looking for in my music. He knows how to blend traditional and contemporary country music and get it to work.

There had been talk about the two of us working together. Eventually, my label reached out to Frank to see if he was interested in working with me. There was one caveat.

"Can you start next week?"

All Frank could do was laugh. We hadn't even met. He's suddenly thinking, *What if I don't like this kid?*

But the train was already moving, and I made plans to visit Frank and get to work. Thankfully, we hit it off right away. It's hard not to like the laid-back family man who has an exceptional ear for music, even if he has bad taste in college sports. But hey, I'll take the Gamecocks over some teams any day.

We've been working off and on this year on the new album. My first single, "Southern Belle," has already been released. It's a different song for me, a fun song with a lot of excitement and one that shows an older Scotty.

Frank's studio sits over his garage. But if you're thinking we're recording between old bikes and rusty tools, think again. This really is *the* place to record or even write songs. The main room is wide and tall and features a wall full of guitars Frank owns and plays. It's the perfect thing to see when you enter. There are couches and a kitchen area, and then the soundboard and computer where Frank and Rich work. I enter the recording booth, which is still roomy enough to move around in and feel comfortable singing inside. There's a window that lets light in and also allows me to see Frank.

We're tracking a song called "Any Other Girl" today. It's a sweet, fun song that sounds and feels good. But the melody still has some tough parts to master.

A lot of songs have already been written for the next album, including several cowritten by me. I try to come into a writing session with ideas. A title or hook, maybe, or even parts of a verse or chorus I've started writing. It tends to make things easier that way.

Some people ask me what comes first—the melody or the lyrics. It kinda just happens all together. It ends up working out. You gotta feel things out and experiment and let the magic happen. It doesn't always happen, of course, but when it does, it's special.

There are other songs Frank and I have heard that we want to record. After picking the demos we've either written or chosen, I'll go to a recording session where I play with the live band. We'll get the raw music down. Then I'm back in the studio a few weeks later to put my vocals on the song. I'll sing the song bit by bit and line by line if I have to, in order to ensure the best possible quality.

I go into the recording booth again and sing for ten seconds. Then do it again. Then again.

"Should you push that second part?" Frank asks me.

I try it again a different way.

"Give me one more of those," he tells me.

With each take recorded, Frank is writing notes on what he's hearing. Rich is behind an iMac computer, making sure everything records right and is where it needs to be.

"One more to make sure we have it really solid," Frank tells me.

I move around and get into each take. Frank will let me keep going when he hears something he likes, but he can also tell when I'm beginning to fade.

"Take thirty seconds," he says.

We'll break, and I'll go into the big room to check my phone and take a sip of room-temperature water. A few minutes later, we're back at it.

Emotion, energy, excitement, feeling—they all gotta be there. The process might be boiled down to a science, but recording is really a unique experience to describe. My voice can sound great but not be right. Frank somehow knows.

Once again, I sing the words of the title.

"Any other girl."

"Okay, try that last line again," Frank says.

"One in a million."

After finishing all the necessary tracking in a day, the song itself might take a week to complete.

"Try one where you hold on to 'to.' "

I try and fail. Try again, and still don't get it right. Frank and Rich chuckle when I come back out again.

"This one's taking it out of you."

When we feel like the track is sufficiently done, we might end up sitting around talking about other ideas for the song.

"You know—there's a really big solo section," Frank says.

"I don't think it needs to be too funked up," I tell them.

"What about an electric guitar?"

More ideas come, and I'm cool with them.

"We could have a guest instrumentalist," I suggest. "Maybe Keith Urban."

> When Scotty comes to the studio to write or record, there are several guarantees you can always count on:
> - His attire will consist of something with the words "NC State" or "Wolfpack."
> - Sports will be a central point of conversation.
> - He will practice his golf swing constantly.
> - He will twirl the headphone cord around his fingers the entire time he sings.
>
> FRANK ROGERS

It's these simple sort of conversations that result in albums having guest appearances. Those are usually done out of courtesy and respect. Sometimes it simply takes Frank or me reaching out to someone and asking.

Yes, it's a business, and yes, it can sometimes even be a cutthroat business. But there's also lots of goodwill and camaraderie that happen on a daily basis. Compared to other genres, country music is like one big family.

After the session, I drive back to where I'm staying and usually think back to the tune I was working on or maybe the next one we'll track.

It's impossible not to be excited about the album. It's months away from release—maybe even half a year—but I'm in the thick of the melodies and lyrics and the stories they tell.

ENOUGH OF THIS TALKING; LET'S GET STARTED

I'm back in Garner and then back in Nashville.

Now I'm back on the road. With my band.

We've been changing up our setlists this year, trying to change things around while having the same structure. The hits are always good—ones like "See You Tonight" and "Feelin' It." But our oldies medley always gets the biggest reaction from the crowd. It's my favorite part of the show too. I love singing some Merle Haggard or Johnny Cash for folks.

Our opening shows for Rascal Flatts are different from our solo shows. Opening for big acts like Brad Paisley or Rascal Flatts are huge opportunities to introduce ourselves to the audience. We have forty minutes to turn them into fans. We try to pack in as big of a punch as we can, keeping the slow tunes to a minimum, with the goal of getting people energized about me and our set.

We know some fans want to hang out and drink beer and have fun at a show. They might be sitting there listening and thinking, *Wasn't that guy on some TV show?* Or they might not even listen at all. But there's always the chance of someone going, "Wow, he's grown up." Or "I never gave him a chance, but he's legit." Someone saying, "Those guys are great."

I usually talk about performances by using the word *we* a lot. The name on the ticket and T-shirt is mine, but once again, there's a band here—and we're all in this thing together.

As the "boss," I'm always remembering this "we thing." This "family thing."

There's Mike with his two boys and two girls.

There's Joey with his three girls.

There's Nathan with his two boys.

It's not just the guys here, but it's also their families and their lives. So it's a pretty cool responsibility to be in this together, doing what we love while earning a living and taking care of those back home.

TRYING TO FIND SOME BALANCE

I love music. It's my passion. But I do enjoy getting away from the music business occasionally to relax and do other things.

I guess that's this thing called balance.

After five years of this journey and after reflecting on it in a book (which isn't an autobiography but more of a travelogue), I can still say I enjoy the music *for the music*. I can honestly say if my career went away tomorrow, I'd still have music. Music will always be a part of me. I'll always have that guitar by my bed, and I know I'll still be content. I'll always have those songs in my head.

Looking ahead to the future, I'd love to have an impact like the greats have had and leave a meaningful legacy. I'd love the heck out of it. I want to make music that will impact lives. My legacy in music isn't going to be defined by number of seats sold or number one hits. It will be defined by what my music says and how it impacts people—whether it's ten people or ten thousand.

After several years on this journey, that desire is still there. The confidence is too, but I think I probably have more self-doubt because of being in this industry. I've seen you can work hard and not have it pay off. But that's life. The journey is as important as the destination. And God has been very good to me. That's why I believe we can do something special.

Chapter Sixteen

Remembering the Moments

I have a song on my upcoming album called "In Between." And it really does represent who I am. This strange dichotomy. "I ain't holy water and I ain't Jim Beam." I'm more comfortable in shorts and T-shirt, unless I'm on the stage or in a meeting. I want the girlfriend, but I'm not quite ready for the ring. Isn't this everyone? Aren't we all in between something?

That's the snapshot right now. What if crazy success happens? Well, I have lots of folks to look at for examples and for wisdom on how to cope. I'm still that kid studying Elvis, listening to Garth, and loving Haggard and Jones and Conway Twitty. That kid is just older now and has a few more responsibilities. I guess that's what getting older is all about.

For now, I'll be in between, working hard and enjoying it.

WHERE I COME FROM

I've talked a lot about how I got here and about my immediate family. Most of this book has been focused on my musical journey. As I said, this isn't an autobiography but more like a record of these last five crazy years. But I can't fail to mention my grandparents and where I really come from.

I've got a lot to be thankful for. I've traveled all over the world, have some college under my belt, own some real estate, and have a little money in the bank. But it's important for folks to know it wasn't always like this in my family. I say this because I've seen you can't let your background and beginnings define you or hold you back.

I've been inspired as I've listened to my grandparents' stories about their lives when they were very young. How they struggled but wanted to make things better for their kids. All of my grandparents were very poor when they were young— whether it was in Bluefield, West Virginia; San Juan, Puerto Rico; or eastern North Carolina.

My granddad Bill grew up in the hills of West Virginia and signed up for the Air Force at age eighteen. My grandma Paquita grew up in old San Juan and talks about watching her mother, my great-grandmother Juanita, go out to the backyard, grab a chicken, and wring its neck before fixing it for supper. Both of my Cooke grandparents grew up on farms in eastern North Carolina—one in Camden County and another near Roanoke Rapids. Each told stories of having oil lamps light their homes at night when they were kids because electricity wasn't available.

My family had very poor beginnings, but each generation got a little more education and encouraged their children to dream a little bigger. Their kids eventually became teachers and state troopers and medical secretaries and members of the military. And lo and behold, one of *their* grandkids actually appeared on television and became a country music singer.

I'm not the only one from the family to see a little success in the entertainment industry. I have a cousin who was a TV news anchor in Ohio. Another cousin in Los Angeles is a comedy writer and filmmaker who created a series that Ron Howard's company is producing. But we all had the same humble beginnings.

My point is—keep pushing and keep following your dreams. Read. Study. Practice. Find what makes you unique. And find someone to push and encourage you along the way. Go big or go home. But most importantly, after you *do* go big, you should also *go home* to thank those people who pushed and encouraged you. Show your love and support to them. Whether it's donating, mentoring, or just being kind, go home after you go big. At least for a little while.

BIRTHDAY BOY

I'm twenty-two today. I'm back in North Carolina hanging out with my boys, the State Eight. These guys have been my friends for a very long time. Some I played baseball with. Most I went to church with, and all of us attended NC State. They came up with the "Flying V," a routine we do when we're out in the public. I'll take the inside center spot, and they form a "V" around me. It helps me slip in and out of places unnoticed.

After a fun and busy birthday weekend of golf and a football game, I'm finishing the weekend with family and friends by the back-yard fire. I guess you know you're getting old when the conversation around the fire centers around politics and the stock market—two topics I enjoy.

So twenty-two years old. What exactly does that mean?

Hard to say. I think the age thing disappeared when I was sixteen and decided to audition for *American Idol* in 2010.

Six years. It's been some kind of six years.

I believe age and time are relative things. A number doesn't define all the things you've learned in life, all the people you've met, and all the places you've been.

Sometimes you'll be somewhere and a song

will come on, taking you back to the first time you heard it. This is one of the powers of music. You can have one singular moment in your life and have a song playing that forever binds you to that song. Then years later, you can walk into a restaurant, hear that song, and think about that special moment and smile.

That's how I feel about *American Idol*. Those songs I sang on *Idol* contain memories that will forever be linked. And if I'm eighty years old one day, I believe I'll still be able to hear a tune and suddenly be transported back to a time and a place and a moment.

So the coolest thing that's happened since I was sixteen? The coolest thing about what I do now? It's not that I get to go on the road and have fun and meet different people and hear my name screamed and see ten thousand fans in front of me. It's not getting paid to do something I love, even though that's such an incredible blessing.

No, I think the coolest thing is knowing I'm helping to create some memories for some of you. Maybe six, ten, or twenty years from now, you'll see my face somewhere and think, *Wow, we had a good time watching him on TV.* Maybe you'll find yourself hearing one of my songs on the radio and remember how much you loved it. Maybe you'll go, "Hey, wasn't he the guy with a low voice on that singing show?" Maybe you won't remember the show's name, and maybe you won't even remember *my* name. But hopefully you'll remember the moment you heard the song and the good times surrounding it.

That's what I hope my music does for you.

Epilogue

The world is full of dreamers. Every now and then, it sends one of its own off into the stars. Looking back, it's been hard to take everything in and comprehend and appreciate all the things happening around me.

It reminds me of one of my new songs I just cowrote—"Five More Minutes."

I've always had this question inside of me.

If you had five more minutes to do anything you wanted at any time of your life with anybody you could think of, what would it be?

Thinking back, it would be hard for me to choose. Really hard to choose. There are so many things I'd love to go back and experience for that short, sweet span of time.

- Five more minutes to sing Elvis tunes on that school bus.
- Five more minutes to sing in my elementary school choir in front of Ms. Palmieri.
- Five more minutes to practice guitar with Gary Epperson.
- Five more minutes on the pitcher's mound at Garner Magnet High.

- Five more minutes to sing with Die Meistersingers and Ms. Clayton.
- Five more minutes to stand before Steven Tyler, Jennifer Lopez, and Randy Jackson.
- Five more minutes to work with Jimmy Iovine and Don Was in the studio.
- Five more minutes to ride in that Mustang next to my parents, feeling the love of my hometown.
- Five more minutes to sing to thirty million Americans watching television.
- Five more minutes on the bus with my band—well, maybe I might get enough of that already.
- Five more minutes to hear Dylan Price play his guitar for me in his hospital room.
- Five more minutes to stand in the Ryman Auditorium and sing a classic.
- Five more minutes to talk with my granddads, Bill McCreery and R. P. Cooke.
- Five more minutes to sit in that baseball stadium with Mom in New Orleans and just watch the game.
- Five more minutes to walk Augusta National with Dad as we head to the Golden Bell to try to make par.

We all want five more minutes, don't we? The great thing is that songs can do that. They can take us back, whether we're singing them or just listening to them. We can hear the memories. We can suddenly be transported.

Life is complicated, but a song can sure make it feel simple. By pressing play and listening for just a few moments, we can put the rest of the world on pause.

Life shouldn't be about looking back, unless it's to thank God for the gifts He's given and to realize how far He's allowed us to come. We can't ever get five minutes of our life back. We can remember them in the music, however. We can replay them and allow them to transport us in sound and lyrics. We can find comfort and joy in the melodies.

Someone once told me, "There are some people who are just born to do something. You're born to sing country music. God blessed with you with that. Don't ever forget it."

I promise I won't forget, Jennifer Lopez. I won't forget all the people who opened doors and pushed me through and kept me moving. A book like this is a reminder of who and for what I'm thankful.

I'm thankful God created songs.

Songs allow us to make sense of the world.

Songs are memories in sound.

All of us have songs in our soul. And some of us—the fortunate and blessed ones—get to sing them out loud and share them with others.

I'll be seeing you in the songs.

Acknowledgments

Even though I'm only twenty-two, there are many people to thank who have helped me on this journey. In the pages of this book, I tried to thank my early teachers back in North Carolina. In more recent years, I want to thank those on different paths in this journey.

I want to thank everyone involved in the television journey, including the *American Idol* team, FremantleMedia, Fox, 19 Entertainment, and, of course, the creator of the show, Simon Fuller of XIX Entertainment. Thank you for being relevant and current and for creating a new way to discover talent and deliver dreams.

After *Idol*, the recording journey began with teams at Interscope and UMG Nashville. Their combined efforts, along with the much-appreciated support from country radio, resulted in a platinum album, a gold album, three platinum singles, and four Top 15 radio hits, including two Top 10 hits.

For the touring and production side of my journey, thanks to Creative Artists Agency and William Morris Endeavor for keeping me in front of the fans. Other key players have included my business managers at FBMM (Flood,

Bumstead, McCready & McCarthy, Inc.); attorneys Don Passman, David Crow, and Bryan Smith; publicists Ebie McFarland and Scott Stem at EBMedia; Crom Tidwell Merchandising; Marbaloo MarkeTing; and the staff at Fan Clubhouse.

Huge thanks to my band and crew of almost a dozen guys *and* our fearless leader—my tour manager, Mike Childers. Thanks for making me look good and having my back these last five years.

This book was made possible by some super-talented professionals. Thanks to my literary agents, Mel Berger and Margaret Riley King, as well as my entire WME team, for helping make me an author. It's been an honor to partner with the great folks at Zondervan, a division of HarperCollins. Special thanks to Jennifer VerHage, Merideth Bliss, Kait Lamphere, Kim Tanner, John Sloan, Dirk Buursma, and Tom Dean. Many thanks also to my cowriter, Travis Thrasher, who became a trusted friend to me and my entire family.

And about my family. A huge shout-out goes to Mike, Judy, and Ashley McCreery, who tolerated the Elvis costumes, late-night guitar strumming, and my singing in every corner of the house. Whether on ball fields, onstage, or on live TV, I know I've caused you multiple heart attacks. Yet you never left my side.

And to my fans, thanks for every tweet, Facebook post, music stream, CD purchase, download, T-shirt, and concert ticket you buy. Your love and support are why I do what I do. I am honored and humbled you enjoy my music.

As you can see, it takes a heck of a lot of people to make the music happen. Thanks again, everyone, for giving me the courage to journey toward the dream.

God bless.

Scotty

SCOTTY MCCREERY: QUICK FACTS

THE BASICS

Birthdate: October 9, 1993
Hometown: Garner, North Carolina
Education: Enrolled at NC State University
                    in 2012
Publicity: Essential Broadcast Media /
                    Scott Stem
Booking: William Morris Endeavor-Nashville
Official Bio: wmeclients.com/music/country
                    /SCOTTY-MCCREERY
Website: www.scottymccreery.com

Promotional Work _____

Bojangles' (twelve states), Cracker Barrel
Country Checkers Challenge,
DoSomething.org/Walmart, Ford, Scout Boats,
and State Farm

Charitable Causes _____

12.14 Foundation, ACM Lifting Lives, American
Red Cross, CMA Foundation, MLB RBI
program, MusiCares, Operation Christmas Child,
Opry Trust Fund, St. Jude Children's Research
Hospital, Waiting for Wishes, and World Vision

MILESTONES

American Idol: Winner of Season 10
               (May 25, 2011)

Albums

- *Clear as Day* (2011)—debuted at #1 on the all-genre Billboard Top 200 Albums Chart (Platinum)
- *Christmas with Scotty McCreery* (2012)—debuted at #1 Billboard Holiday Albums Chart (Gold)
- *See You Tonight* (2013)—debuted at #1 Billboard Country Albums Chart

Singles

- *I Love You This Big* (2011)—Platinum (Top 15 radio hit)
- *The Trouble With Girls* (2011)—Platinum (Top 15 radio hit)
- *Water Tower Town* (2012)
- *See You Tonight* (2013)—Platinum (Top 10 radio hit)
- *Feelin' It* (2014) —Gold (Top 10 radio hit)

Industry Awards and Recognition

- 2011 Academy of Country Music (ACM): *Best New Artist*

- 2011 American Country Awards (ACA): *New Artist of the Year*
- 2012 CMT Music Awards: *Breakthrough Video of the Year* (*The Trouble With Girls*)
- 2013 Inspirational Country Music Awards: *Mainstream Country Male Artist*
- 2013 American Country Awards (ACA): *Breakthrough Artist of the Year*
- Billboard *21 Under 21 ~ Music's Hottest Young Stars (2011–2014)*
- BMI Award for Writing One of the Top 50 Country Songs of 2015 ("See You Tonight")
- Voted "Country's Sexiest Man" by the readers of *NASH Country Weekly Magazine* in 2015
- Voted "Best American Idol" by the readers of *The Los Angeles Times* in February 2016

Center Point Large Print
600 Brooks Road / PO Box 1
Thorndike, ME 04986-0001 USA

(207) 568-3717

US & Canada:
1 800 929-9108
www.centerpointlargeprint.com